UFOS

AND THE

SUPERNATURAL

Ken Hudnall
Omega Press
El Paso, Texas

UFOs And The Supernatural

Copyright © 2012 Ken Hudnall

All rights reserved. No part of this book may be reproduced or transmitted in any form or by any means, graphic, electronic, or mechanical, including photocopying, recording, taping or by any information storage or retrieval system, without the permission in writing from the publisher.

OMEGA PRESS
An Imprint of Omega Communications Group, Inc.

For Information address:

Omega Press
5823 N. Mesa, #839
El Paso, Texas 79912

Or

http://www.kenhudnall.com

First Edition

Printed in the United States of America

OTHER WORKS BY THE SAME AUTHOR UNDER THE NAME KEN HUDNALL

SERIES
MANHATTAN CONSPIRACY
Blood on the Apple
Capital Crimes
Angel of Death
Confrontation

THE OCCULT CONNECTION
U.F.O.S, Secret Societies and Ancient Gods
The Hidden Race
Unidentified Flying Objects
Secret Societies
Ancient Gods

DARKNESS
When Darkness Falls
Fear The Darkness
Defy The Darkness

SPIRITS OF THE BORDER
The History and Mystery of El Paso Del Norte
The History and Mystery of Fort Bliss, Texas
The History and Mystery of The Rio Grande
Tales From The Nightshift
El Paso: A City of Secrets
Echoes of the Past
The History and Mystery of New Mexico
The History and Mystery of the Lone Star State
The History and Mystery of Arizona
The History and Mystery of Tombstone, Arizona
The History and Mystery of Colorado
Restless Spirits
Military Ghosts

School Spirits
The History and Mystery of Sin City
The History and Mystery of Northeast Texas

<u>THE ESTATE SALE MURDERS</u>
Dead Man's Diary
Curse of the Dragon's Tooth
A Bloody Afternoon of Fun

Footprints In The Sand

Seventy Years and No Losses

Even Paranoids Have Enemies

Veterans Practical Primer

Where No Car Has Gone Before

Knights of the Golden Circle

Lost Treasures of the Confederacy

Making Money From Information

Lost Padre Mine

Lost and Buried Treasures of Texas

How Not To Get Published

Language of the Law

Criminal Law For Laymen

Understanding Business Law

The History of ASARCO

As ROBERT K. HUDNALL

No Safe Haven: Homeland Insecurity

The Northwood Conspiracy

DEDICATION

As with all of my books, the one whose support has been most important to the completion of the project has been my lovely wife, Sharon. Without her assistance, all of my ideas would remain just ideas. I would also dedicated this book to those who have had contact with the UFOs and not been believed.

Contents

THOSE WHO TO EARTH CAME 9

ATTEMPS TO EXPLAIN UNIDENTIFIED FLYING OBJECTS 25

ALIEN LOVERS AND OTHER CREATURES . 35

SECRETS 47

A CLOSER LOOK AT EZEKIAL'S WHEEL 61

MEN FROM THE SHADOWS 71

OTHER INSTANCES OF ALIEN INVOLVEMENT 97

DIRECT INTERVENTION 107

NON-HUMANS AMONG US 123

AGENTS OF THE UNSEEN 145

THE MASTERS 161

UNIDENTIFIED FLYING OBJECTS AND

SASQUATCH 211

AND THEN 225

INDEX 227

CHAPTER ONE
THOSE WHO TO EARTH CAME

This work is designed to look beyond the obvious, to delve into realms that are only sensed but never proven. This is a work that studies the possibility that the world of the supernatural may well be involved with the question of the reality of what we call unidentified flying objects. There have been many stories of unidentified flying objects that have a definite supernatural aspect to them. So if these strange lights in the sky are all craft from another world, then how can they have aspects that tend to involve what we refer to as the supernatural?

However, before investigating how unidentified flying objects and the supernatural are related, we first need to have a working definition for the term supernatural. One

Figure 1: A common image in reported UFO sightings.

of the best definitions for supernatural that I have found comes from Merriam-webster.com[1]. According to these experts in the meanings of language, supernatural means:

- of or relating to an order of existence beyond the visible observable universe; especially: of or relating to God or a god, demigod, spirit, or devil, or
- a: departing from what is usual or normal especially so as to appear to transcend the laws of nature or b: attributed to an invisible agent (as a ghost or spirit)

I am sure at this point, the reader is chuckling at the very idea that what most believe are craft from an advanced race can have anything to do with the gods of history, ghosts, hauntings or the paranormal. Well you would be wrong. After all, if UFOs are space craft and the pilots are real beings, then what possible connection can they have with the paranormal?

Figure 2: The world of the paranormal.

It is the premise of this work that what we refer to as unidentified flying objects are, in fact, made by entities who came to this earth to take advantage of both the resources here as well as the natives. Using their advanced scientific knowledge, these entities set themselves up as gods and ruled over mankind for many thousands of years. The question is what was their ultimate purpose? If, as it

---

[1] http://www.merriam-webster.com/dictionary/supernatural

appears, they have been here for tens of thousands and perhaps hundreds of thousands of years, what did they hope to achieve? Well, as we move further into this work, perhaps we can discover the purpose behind it all.

Teachers and Others

There have long been stories of mysterious teachers and mentors seemingly appearing out of the shadows, giving guidance to humans. Some believe that they are survivors of earlier, more advanced earth civilizations, such as Atlantis, and others believe they are aliens from another world. It is interesting to note that there are many researchers who believe that another world does not have to be another planet, but could also be another dimension.

There is no question that there were a number of ancient teachers who were said to have taught various cultures the basics of civilization. In Sumeria there was Oannes, who is discussed below and others of his kind. In South America there was Quetzalcoatl, also known as the feathered serpent. He allegedly left South America to sail to his homeland located in the east. Was he from an advanced society with the mission of teaching primitives or was he a representative of an alien culture. Either way, he and others like him had a major impact on the civilizations that began on earth and are considered gods by many to this day.

Ancient UFOs

Many people seem to believe that the appearance of unidentified flying objects began around July of 1947. This is the time frame when businessman Kenneth Arnold saw his mysterious

Figure 3: Headline based on a military press release.

flying disks near Mount Rainier and when many believe that a flying saucer crashed near the town of Roswell, New Mexico. This is most definitely not true. Unidentified flying objects have been around since before the appearance of mankind and it appears that the occupants have been meddling in human affairs almost as long.

Figure 4: St. Peters Basilica

One example would be the Sumerian tales regarding Oannes, said to have been the one to teach the rudiments of civilization to the ancient Sumerians. Of course, Oannes did not have to be from another planet. Many said that the most likely scenario, if Oannes was indeed a historical figure, is that Oannes was a traveler from another part of the globe, from a pre-existing civilization yet to be discovered.

According to early Sumerian records, "A man, or rather a monster, Half man and half fish, coming from the sea, appeared near Babylon; he had two heads; one, which was the highest, resembled that of man, the other that of a fish. He had the feet of a man and the tail of a fish; and his speech and voice resembled that of a man: a representation of him is still preserved. This monster dwelt by day with men, but took no food; he gave them knowledge of letters, arts, and sciences; he taught them to build towers and temples; and to establish laws; he instructed them in the principles of geometry; taught them to sow, and to gather the fruits of the earth; in short, whatever could contribute to polish and civilize their manners. At sun set he retired to the sea, in which he passed the night. There appeared likewise others of the same species."

Religious Belief – An Alien Concept?

Assuming for a moment that these early visitors came to conquer the planet, how many ships and soldiers would have been needed to subjugate every humanoid on this planet? I would submit that this would be an impossible job. However, if these mysterious visitors could establish in the minds of the early inhabitants of this planet that the visitors had a "right" to exploit this planet by virtue of being the gods that created everything, their job would be simple. This religious belief could be used to control the human race through the use of taboos, which are found in almost every society, past as well as in the present.

Early man was a blank slate just waiting for some entity to write on it. Anything that could not be explained was thought by early man to have been caused by a god or goddess or some other invisible force. As a result, it was easy for any advanced race to convince the primitive races of this planet that they were gods. Science fiction author Arthur C. Clarke's[2] third law states "Any sufficiently advanced technology is indistinguishable from magic." Thus convincing the primitive locals that you are a god is not hard.

---

[2] Clarke's Three Laws are three "laws" of prediction formulated by the British writer and scientist Arthur C. Clarke. They are:
 1. When a distinguished but elderly scientist states that something is possible, he is almost certainly right. When he states that something is impossible, he is very probably wrong.
 2. The only way of discovering the limits of the possible is to venture a little way past them into the impossible.
 3. Any sufficiently advanced technology is indistinguishable from magic.

Figure 5: Every religion has symbols that evoke fear and awe

While this work is not a treatise on religion, it will assist our true goal to do an overview of the topic. That being said, it is best to start with a definition.

Religion is a collection of cultural systems, belief systems, and worldviews that relate humanity to spirituality and, sometimes, to moral values. Many religions have narratives, symbols, traditions and sacred histories that are intended to give meaning to life or to explain the origin of life or the universe. They tend to derive morality, ethics, religious laws or a preferred lifestyle from their ideas about the cosmos and human nature.

The word religion is sometimes used interchangeably with faith or belief system, but religion differs from private belief in that it has a public aspect. Thus, a private belief, no matter how fervently held is not a religion. Some religions have organized behaviors, clergy, a definition of what constitutes adherence or membership, congregations of laity, regular meetings or services for the purposes of veneration of a deity or for prayer, holy places (either natural or architectural), and/or scriptures.

The practice of a religion may also include sermons, commemoration of the activities of a god or gods, sacrifices, festivals, feasts, trance, initiations, funerary services, matrimonial services, meditation, music, art, dance, public service, or other aspects of human culture. However, there are examples of religions for which some or many of these aspects of structure, belief, or practices are absent.

The development of religion has taken different forms in different cultures. Some religions place an emphasis on having a certain belief, while others emphasize practice, such as Muslims who pray many times per day. Some religions focus on the subjective experience of the religious individual, while others consider the activities of the religious community to be most important. Some religions claim to be universal, believing their laws and cosmology to be binding for everyone, while others are intended to be practiced only by a closely defined or localized group.

In many places religion has been associated with public institutions such as education, hospitals, the family, government, and political hierarchies. Anthropologists John Monoghan and Peter Just state that, "it seems apparent that one thing religion or belief helps us do is deal with problems of human life that are significant, persistent, and intolerable. One important way in which religious beliefs accomplish this is by providing a set of ideas about how and why the world is put together that allows people to accommodate anxieties and deal with misfortune."

Some academics studying the subject have divided religions into three broad categories: world religions, a term which refers to transcultural, international faiths; indigenous religions, which refers to smaller, culture-specific or nation-specific religious groups; and new

Figure 6: Classic Alien Grey

religious movements, which refers to recently developed faiths.

One modern academic theory of religion, social constructionism, says that religion is a modern concept that suggests all spiritual practice and worship follows a model similar to the Abrahamic religions as an orientation system that helps to interpret reality and define human beings, and thus religion, as a concept, has been applied inappropriately to non-Western cultures that are not based upon such systems, or in which these systems are a substantially simpler construct.

One common denominator found in every religion is that the god, or gods, that are worshipped invariably work miracles. In response to this, I refer the reader to Clark's Third Law quoted above.

Setting the Stage

Before we discuss how unidentified flying objects and the world of the supernatural interact, we must first determine what we are dealing with. So we need to determine exactly what do when mean when we talk about unidentified flying objects. In other words exactly what are UFOs?

While there has been no definitive answer to this question, the UFO phenomenon has been with us for thousands of years, even though many believe the UFO era began with the Kenneth Arnold sightings in 1947. Proponents of the ancient astronaut theories often maintain

Figure 7: Did aliens build the pyramids?

that humans are either descendants of early alien visitors or perhaps artificial creations of extraterrestrial beings who landed on Earth thousands of years ago. A prime example of these ideas can be found in the works of Zecharia Sitchin whose series The Earth Chronicles, revolves around Sitchin's interpretation of ancient Sumerian and Middle Eastern texts, megalithic sites, and artifacts from around the world.

The premise that the Human Race is the descendant of ancient astronauts gives rise to the associated idea is that much of human knowledge, religion, and culture came from these extraterrestrial visitors in ancient times, in that ancient astronauts acted as a "mother culture" or a mentoring intelligence. Ancient astronaut proponents such as Erich von Däniken also believe that travelers from outer space built many of the ancient structures on earth such as the pyramids in Egypt.

Figure 8: One of many ancient clues showing ancient astronauts

Supporters of these theories argue that the evidence for ancient astronauts comes from unexplained gaps in historical and archaeological records, as well as ancient myths and legends and that absent historical or archaeological data that can explain these gaps, the existence of ancient astronauts is a valid premise. The evidence is said to include archaeological artifacts that they argue are anachronistic or beyond the presumed technical capabilities of the historical cultures with which they are associated; and there is also artwork and legends which are interpreted as depicting extraterrestrial contact or technologies such as some of the carvings on the Gateway to the Sun.

Of course in response to these theories, mainstream academics have responded that gaps in contemporary knowledge of the past need not demonstrate that such speculative ancient astronaut ideas are a necessary conclusion to draw. However, there are also mainstream academics such as Francis Crick, the co-discoverer of the double helix structure of DNA, who strongly believed in what he called panspermia, the concept that earth was 'seeded' with life, probably in the form of blue green algae, by intelligent extraterrestrial species, for the purpose of ensuring life's continuity. He believed that this could have been done on any number of planets of this class, possibly using unmanned shuttles.

Figure 9: One reported form of UFO abduction.

Another mainstream academic, Thomas Gold, a professor of astronomy, suggested a "garbage theory" for the origin of life, proposing that life on earth might have spread from a pile of waste products accidentally dumped on Earth long ago by extraterrestrials. Other researchers have suggested that the earth many have been a prison planet, which would explain many things about the human race, or perhaps the site of a crash and from the survivors came Adam and Eve. The theories are endless.

Whatever your belief system, this topic has been a fertile area for both education and entertainment. The television series Ancient Aliens on the History channel features the main proponents in the ancient astronaut theory, and has included interviews with such leaders in the field as Giorgio A. Tsoukalos, David Hatcher Childress, Erich von Däniken, Steven Greer and Nick Pope.

If the human race as we know it came from the interference, or perhaps, manipulation by alien races in the development of the inhabitants of this planet, that is astounding, but how can the supernatural play a part in what would seem to be a very simple concept? This will come out as we continue.

Abductions

One aspect of the UFO phenomenon that has disturbed many is the so called abductions of humans by so called alien entities. We often see alien abduction as a contemporary phenomenon, happening mostly in the last sixty or seventy years with a few trace cases reaching back into antiquity all the way to the middle ages. However, this may not be the case.

Figure 10: One example of Tassili rock paintings

Examination of cave paintings left by early inhabitants of the Tassili[3] region in North Africa suggests the phenomenon may be far older and more widespread than we ever understood before. Were there cases of ancient alien abductions in ancient times? The evidence would seem to support this idea.

Some of the rock paintings on the Tassili plateau, which have been photographed and written about a number of times, depict a woman being led by mysterious figures toward a large spherical object located nearby. The creatures involved look roughly humanoid except for a helmet which appears very similar to one commonly described by witnesses as an extraterrestrial space helmet.

The level of technology shown in these rock paintings is far simpler than verbal reports, with the alleged creatures requiring breathing apparatus or some sort of

---

[3] Tassili n'Ajjer (Berber: Tasili n Ajjer, meaning "Plateau of the Rivers") is a mountain range in the Algerian section of the Sahara Desert. It is a vast plateau in south-east Algeria at the borders of Libya, Niger and Mali, covering an area of 72,000 sq. km.

The range is also noted for its prehistoric rock art and other ancient archaeological sites, dating from Neolithic times when the local climate was much moister, with savannah rather than desert. The art depicts herds of cattle, large wild animals including crocodiles, and human activities such as hunting and dancing. The art has strong stylistic links to the pre-Nguni Art of South Africa and the region, executed in caves by the San Peoples before the year 1200 BCE. There is also a strong link to the Serer people of Senegal, the Gambia and Mauritania, where rupestral engravings depicts the symbol of the Pangool (ancient Serer saints and ancestral spirits in Serer religion) around 10,000 BCE].

The range's exceptional density of rock art paintings-pictograms and engravings-petroglyphs, and the presence of many prehistoric vestiges, are remarkable testimonies to Neolithic prehistory. From 10,000 BCE to the first centuries CE, successive peoples left many archaeological remains, habitations, burial mounds and enclosures which have yielded abundant lithic and ceramic material. However, it is the rock art (engravings and paintings) that have made Tassili world famous beginning in 1933, the date of its discovery. More than 15,000 petroglyphs have been identified to date.

space helmet - possibly in order to survive Earth's atmosphere. The woman in the painting is depicted with no exaggerated features, simply as a human figure being led by the hand. Was this a scene the painter saw with his own eyes; the details would make it appear to be the case?

Looking back throughout history, however, there are several cases where beings from somewhere else - often the sky or deep underground have taken humans captive. Occasionally these people are returned to tell their tale, but other times those taken are never seen again.

So here we have evidence from a very desolate area that humans were sometimes chosen to interact with very real members of a more advanced race, those we might call aliens. But is the all of the evidence of such contact? Not by a long shot. In fact one of the most read books in the world is full of tails of contact between humans and aliens. That book is the Holy Bible.

Ezekiel's Wheel

Skeptics have long complained that there is no definitive proof of alien intervention with humans. However, from the Biblical Old Testament, chapter 1 of the Book of Ezekiel believers in the ancient alien phenomenon often point to the story of Ezekiel's wheel in which Ezekiel saw several mysterious creatures aboard what he described as a wheel which was raising and lowering in the sky. Was Ezekiel's wheel a simpler interpretation of the more modern flying saucer from someone who was not familiar with technology?

A NASA engineer by the name of Josef F. Blumrich, decided to get to the bottom of this mystery and the result was a book entitled *"The Spaceships of Ezekiel"*[4]. This book concluded that the familiar Biblical passages in the Book of Ezekiel weren't the whole story of this

---

[4] Blumrich, Josef F., The Spaceships of Ezekiel, Corgi, 1974.

incident. Blumrich agrees that the "wheel within a wheel" was extraterrestrial, but he goes one step further and claims that it only describes a small part of the craft. According to Blumrich, this entire Biblical chapter of Ezekiel was a detailed description of an encounter with an UFO.

Even the story behind the book is very interesting. Blumrich notes that he began researching the topic in response to Erich von Däniken book *Chariots of the Gods*[5]. In the forward to his book, Blumrich states that he "began to read von Däniken with the condescending attitude of someone who knows beforehand that the conclusions presented can by no means be correct." In other words, he thought von Däniken was wrong and he set out to prove it scientifically.

What he found, after an extensive amount of research from an engineering point of view, was just the opposite. He went from an extreme skeptic to becoming convinced that the Book of Ezekiel was an accurate and detailed account of an encounter with extraterrestrial visitors. Very interesting coming from a person who is not a religious zealot by any means and is about as far as you can get from a gullible person who might be prone to jump to conclusions.

Even though many mainstream scientists are unable to accept that advanced races have been here for thousands

---

[5] Von Däniken, Eric, Chariots of the Gods, Bantam Books, 1972.

of years, the evidence is strong in support of that premise. So here we have the UFO or unidentified flying object, arguably a real vehicle, the result of advanced technology. So now how does the concept of the supernatural become involved?

24

CHAPTER TWO
ATTEMPS TO EXPLAIN
UNIDENTIFIED FLYING OBJECTS

There are a number of hypotheses regarding unidentified flying objects that seem to cover the gamut. Many different ideas have been proposed to try and explain the reported phenomena and nature of UFOs. None of these ideas are new, in fact they can be found through the literature as well as on the internet. A quick review of these ideas seems to be in order before we look at our last proposal regarding Ghosts and hauntings.

UFOs Are From Other Planets
What might be termed the extraterrestrial hypothesis (ETH) was defined by Edward U. Condon in the 1968 Condon Report as "The idea that some UFOs may be spacecraft sent to Earth from another civilization or on a planet associated with a more distant star".

The idea that UFOs came from another planet was first made popular by investigator and author Donald Keyhoe's in his UFO book from 1950[6], though the idea clearly predated Keyhoe, having already appeared in

---

[6] Keyhoe, Donald E, Flying Saucers From Outer Space, Arrow Books, 1950.

newspaper stories and various government documents.

The idea that UFOs come from another planet is probably the most popular theory among Ufologists. Some private or governmental studies, some secret, have concluded in favor of the ETH, or have had members who disagreed with official conclusions against the conclusion by committees and agencies to which they belonged.

UFOs are Hostile

What is referred to as the UFO Hostility Hypothesis is actually included within the extraterrestrial hypothesis. This concept proposes that the extraterrestrial beings that travel in the UFOs, or most of them, are hostile to humans.

The hypothesis comes because of the Cattle Mutilations and the observations made by Wilhelm Reich and Jerome Eden during their experiments with the Cloudbuster.

UFOs are Electromagnetic Balls of Light

The theory that UFOs can be explained by electromagnetic balls of plasma can be traced back to the work of Philip J. Klass in the 1960s who wanted to find a natural explanation for UFOs. Klass worked hard to debunk the entire concept of UFOs and was able to show that in certain cases there was evidence that UFOs sightings could be explained by balls of plasma and that UFOs were not extraterrestrial in origin.

Some later researchers concluded that there was a strong link between UFO sightings and high levels of solar activity. This idea was later confirmed by another researcher in 1980. Another study to support this hypothesis was carried out by Jacques Vallée. Vallée completed an analysis on a large number of UFO sighting reports and found that in almost all cases the events started with the perception of a light. These findings added credibility to the hypothesis that balls of light and UFOs are linked. The British government commissioned an official report on UFOs in 2000 which concluded that that UFOs are balls of electromagnetic plasma.

Peter F. Coleman later advanced a theory that some UFOs may be explained by fireballs, instances of visible combustion of a fuel (e. g., natural gas) inside an atmospheric vortex. Australian astrophysicist Stephen Hughes has also claimed there is evidence that some UFOs can be explained by ball lightning.

UFOs are Earthlights

Related to the balls of light hypothesis is the idea of earthlights or earthquake lights hypothesis which is based on the work of various independent researchers who have attempted to link UFO sightings where geological faults and geomagnetic fluctuations occur. Early researchers to suggest this hypothesis included Charles Fort, John Keel and Ferdinand Lagarde.

Paul Devereux in 1982 had published an important work advocating the Earthlights hypothesis. Michael Persinger in the late 1980s also published a number of research findings in scientific journals and a book (Persinger and Lafrenière 1977) which attempted to link psychological and neurological dimensions of UFOs sightings with geomagnetic activities. Egon Bach author of UFOs from the Volcanoes (1993) also supported the hypothesis linking the phenomena to tornadoes and volcanoes.

UFOs Are Electromagnetic Manifestations

The electromagnetic hypothesis can be traced to the work of independent researchers such as Michael Persinger who have claimed that electromagnetism can affect human perception. The hypothesis claims that if the human brain is exposed to high levels of electromagnetism then it can disturb the normal processes of the brain and cause altered states of consciousness, hallucinations and types of visionary experience. Persinger claims this may explain some UFO sightings as well as other paranormal phenomena. Persinger has also linked geomagnetism to paranormal phenomena. Other researchers have confirmed the work of Persinger that the human mind can become influenced by electromagnetism and lead to paranormal effects.

A notable advocate of the electromagnetic hypothesis is Albert Budden author of the book Electric UFOs (1998)[7]. Budden calls his hypothesis the "electro-staging hypothesis"; he claims that electromagnetic fields can induce hallucinations which can appear very realistic to the witness.

UFOs are Interdimensional

The interdimensional hypothesis (IDH or IH), also called the extra dimensional hypothesis (EDH), is a theory advanced by Jacques Vallée that says unidentified flying objects (UFOs) and related events involve visitations from other "realities" or "dimensions" that coexist separately alongside our own. It is an alternative to the extraterrestrial hypothesis (ETH).

The French author Jacques Vallée believes that UFO sightings have strong links to supernatural creatures like fairies and elves, religious apparitions, and that they all emerge suddenly from a neighboring reality or dimension. The old reports of these "little people" are found very similar to experiences like lapses of missing time, people disappearing and popping in unexpected places, and modern UFO abductions. States Vallée, "we are dealing with a yet unrecognized level of consciousness, independent of man but closely linked to the Earth."

---

[7] Budden, Albert, Electric UFOs, Cassell Illustrated (September 3, 1998)

IDH also holds that UFOs are a modern manifestation of a phenomenon that has occurred throughout recorded human history, which in prior ages was ascribed to mythological or supernatural creatures. Meade Layne had proposed an early version of the interdimensional hypothesis to explain flying saucer sightings. He speculated that, rather than representing advanced military or extraterrestrial technology, flying saucers were piloted by beings from a parallel dimension, which he called Etheria, and their "ether ships" were usually invisible but could be seen when their atomic motion became slow enough. He further claimed that Etherians could become stranded on the terrestrial plane when their ether ships malfunctioned and that various governments were aware of these incidents and had investigated them.

Although ETH has remained the predominant explanation for UFOs by Ufologists, some Ufologists have abandoned it in favor of IDH. Paranormal researcher Brad Steiger wrote that "we are dealing with a multidimensional paraphysical phenomenon that is largely indigenous to planet Earth". Other Ufologists, such as John Ankerberg and John Weldon, advocate IDH because it fits the explanation of UFOs as a spiritistic phenomenon. Commenting on the disparity between the ETH and the accounts that people have made of UFO encounters, Ankerberg and Weldon wrote "the UFO phenomenon simply does not behave like extraterrestrial visitors." In the book UFOs: Operation Trojan Horse published in 1970, John Keel linked UFOs to supernatural concepts such as ghosts and demons.

Also Jerome Clark was influenced by IDH but then he rejected this hypothesis and argued very cautiously in favor of the extraterrestrial hypothesis.

The development of IDH as an alternative to ETH increased in the 1970s and 1980s with the publication of books by Vallée and J. Allen Hynek. In 1975, Vallée and Hynek advocated the hypothesis in The Edge of Reality: A Progress Report on Unidentified Flying Objects and further, in Vallée's 1979 book Messengers of Deception: UFO Contacts and Cults[8].

UFOs Are Cryptoterrestrial Creatures
The Cryptoterrestrial hypothesis was suggested by the ufologist and futurologist Mac Tonnies. It concentrates on the idea that the so called extraterrestrial intelligence is not out of our planet, but living among us.

UFOs Are Paranormal In Nature
Some early psychical researchers such as Gustav Geley speculated that paranormal phenomena could be explained by the human mind materializing objects this view had influenced a minority of UFO investigators in the 1970s. In 1975, John Keel published the Mothman Prophecies[9]s based on his investigation of reported UFOs in West Virginia. Keel had linked poltergeists and other paranormal events to the UFO sightings which he claimed were all occurring at the same.
Another researcher Karl Brunstein in 1979 proposed similar ideas linking UFO sightings to paranormal events. Other researchers also pointed out that there were similar features of reported sightings of ghosts and apparitions to UFOs. The parapsychologist D. Scott Rogo also linked paranormal phenomena with UFO sightings, however the majority of parapsychologists do not study UFOs and very few advocate the hypothesis.

---

[8] (New Edition) Vallée, Jacques, Messengers of Deception: UFO Contacts and Cults, Daily Grail Publishing; American edition (June 1, 2008)
[9] Keel John, The Mothman Prophecies, Tor Books; 1st edition (February 18, 2002) (Mass Market edition)

John Spencer in his book *Gifts of the Gods: Are UFOs Alien Visitors or Psychic Phenomena?*[10] (1994) claimed that ufological and paranormal events are the outcome of a natural force or energy that science has not yet detected.

UFOs Are An Atmospheric Life Form

The Atmospheric life form hypothesis also known as the "Space Animal", "Space Critter" or "Sky Beast" hypothesis claims that UFOs are living organisms from the Earth's atmosphere. The Naturalist Ivan T. Sanderson was supportive of the hypothesis in his book Uninvited Visitors (1967)[11] and independently in the same year the paranormal writer Vincent Gaddis had also advocated the hypothesis in his book Mysterious Fires and Lights[12] (1967). Kenneth Arnold was also a proponent of the hypothesis and wrote that UFOs are "groups and masses of living organisms that are as much a part of our atmosphere and space as the life we find in the oceans."

The UFO researcher John Philip Bessor believed that UFOs originate from the atmosphere and are "living organisms, sort of like sky jellyfish". Zoe Wassilko-Serecki an Austrian noblewoman wrote a number of articles in an occult magazine in which she concluded that UFOs were life forms in the atmosphere which feed on pure energy, creating "bladder-like bodies for themselves out of colloidal silicones." A famous reporting of a "sky beast" was the Crawfordsville monster which was sighted in Indiana in 1891.

Another early UFO writer Trevor James Constable believed that the UFO phenomenon was best explained by

---

[10] Spencer, John, Gifts of the Gods? Are UFOs Alien Visitors or Psychic Phenomena?, Virgin, 1994.
[11] Sanderson, Ivan T., Uninvited Visitors, Tandem (1974).
[12] Gaddis, Vincent, Mysterious Fires and Lights, Borderland Sciences Research Foundation (1994)

the presence of large amoeba-like animals inhabiting Earth's atmosphere. He called these hypothetical creatures "critters." Constable speculated that they spent most of their time in an invisible low-density state and propelled themselves through the air with "orgonic energy, a force common to all living creatures".

Constable wrote that UFOs "are amoeba like life-forms existing in the plasma state. They are not solid, liquid, or gas. Rather, they exist in the fourth state of matter—plasma—as living heat-substance..." He believed when they increased their density, the animals became visible. He thought that "critters" were carnivores and the mutilated animal carcasses and unexplained disappearances were evidence that they sometimes preyed on humans and livestock. The implementation of radar was theorized to be the reason that the critters were being seen more often, as Constable imagined that it disturbs them out of hiding. Constable developed his ideas in two books The Cosmic Pulse of Life (1977)[13] and Sky Creatures: Living UFOs (1978)[14] in these books also appeared photographs of which he claimed were evidence for "critters".

Another researcher the hydrophone inventor John M. Cage theorized that UFOs are sentient life-forms that follow airplanes, he wrote that UFOs are "sentient life forms of a highly tenuous composition, charged with and feeding upon electricity in the form of negative electricity."

The hypothesis was mentioned in detail by the cryptozoologist Karl Shuker in his book Dr. Shuker's Casebook (2008)[15].

---

[13] Constable, Trevor James, The Cosmic Pulse of Life, TBS The Book Service Ltd (September 15, 1977)
[14] Constable, Trevor James, Pocket (May 1, 1978).
[15] Shuker, Karl, Dr. Shuker's Casebook, cfz (August 1, 2008).

Psychosocial hypothesis

The psychosocial or psychocultural hypothesis, colloquially abbreviated (PSH) or (PCH), argues that at least some UFO reports are best explained by psychological or social means. It is often contrasted with the better known extraterrestrial hypothesis (ETH), and is particularly popular among UFO researchers in the United Kingdom, such as David Clarke, Hilary Evans, the editors of Magonia Magazine, and many of the contributors to Fortean Times Magazine. It is also popular in France since the publication in 1977 of a book written by Michel Monnerie, Et si les ovnis n'existaient pas? (What if ufos do not exist?).

Ufologists claim that the psychocultural hypothesis is occasionally confused with aggressive anti-ETH debunking, but that there is an important difference in that the PCH researcher sees UFOs as an interesting subject that is worthy of serious study, even if it is approached in a skeptical (i.e. non-credulous) way.[66]

The paradox of science fiction UFOs

Several authors underline the fact that the science-fiction magazines, stories, etc., curiously predate the UFO phenomena. Bertrand Méheust, a French sociologist, in his 1978 book Science-fiction et soucoupes volantes (Science-Fiction and flying saucers), claimed that almost every aspect of the UFO phenomena can be located in pulp magazines of the beginning of the 20th century, well before the beginning of the modern UFO phenomena around 1947.

In the same vein, in his article The truth is: They never were saucers, Robert Sheaffer argued that just after the Kenneth Arnold case, most witnesses described UFOs as saucer- shaped, which agrees with the "flying saucer" reports in the media coverage of the event, but allegedly disagreed with what Arnold himself reported seeing, claiming Arnold instead reported "flying boomerangs." Sheaffer then argued that this type of phenomenon demonstrates the importance of the culture in UFO narratives.

Mass hysteria

Some authors have argued that the UFO phenomena show aspects of a mass hysteria, especially during UFO Waves. The French psychiatrist George Heuyer wrote this hypothesis in 1954 in a note to the Bulletin de l'Académie Nationale de Médecine.

History of the PSH

With his essay 'Flying Saucers: A Modern Myth of Things Seen in the Skies (1958), Carl Gustav Jung can be seen as one of the founding father of the PSH. On the other hand, because of his use of the concept of synchronicity in this book, he is also one of the founding father of paranormal explanations of the UFO phenomena.

However, even though Jung at times advanced the idea that UFOs might be partly psychological manifestations, he was also on record stating that some might be true physical objects under intelligent control, citing in particular radar corroboration. Jung also seriously considered the Extraterrestrial Hypothesis. For example, Associated Press quoted him in 1958 saying, "a purely psychological explanation is ruled out." The flying saucers were real and "show signs of intelligent guidance and quasi-human pilots. I can only say for certain that these things are not a mere rumor, something has been seen. ...If the extraterrestrial origin of these phenomena should be confirmed, this would prove the existence of an intelligent interplanetary relationship. ...That the construction of these machines proves a scientific technique immensely superior to ours cannot be disputed."

Hilary Evans was a notable exponent of the psychosocial hypothesis of UFOs as culturally shaped visionary experiences.

CHAPTER THREE
ALIEN LOVERS AND OTHER CREATURES

And There Were Giants in Those Days

Now comes the good stuff. There would seem to be no doubt that someone has been messing with the human race. I guess the opposite of an alien abduction would be an alien moving in and living among us humans. There is another account in the Bible that seems to describe alien visitation that led to what might be called an invasion of sorts; this one coming from the Book of Matthew that described the B'nai Elohim that took as wives the daughters of Adam and brought forth a race of powerful beings which are said to have existed alongside

Figure 11: The skeletons of giants have been found over the years.

the human race from its earliest stages.

Is this a purely apocryphal tale? Or does it describe the presence of an ancient race of beings engaged in the same genetic gathering practices that are spoken of today in alien abduction accounts? According to the Book of Matthew when men began to multiply on earth and daughters were born to them, the sons of heaven saw how beautiful the daughters of man were, and so they took for their wives as many as they chose.

Figure 12: Evidence of giants is wide spread.

Then the Lord said: *'My spirit shall not remain in man forever, since he is flesh. His days shall comprise one hundred and twenty years.'*

This pairing of aliens and human females resulted in the appearance of what we might term as a hybrid which was called the Nephilim on earth. According to the scripture, after the sons of heaven had intercourse with daughters of man, they bore them sons who were heroes of old, the men of renown.

In the Book of Genesis it indicates that the "sons of God" (termed

Figure 13: Representation of El is at top of relic.

the B'nai Elohim in Hebrew) took wives of the "daughters of men." This coupling spawned the "Nephilim." The B'nai Elohim is a term that refers to angelic beings. B'nai is Semitic meaning Son and Elohim is a curiously plural name for the Hebrew deity opposed to the singular Yahweh.

This early genetic breeding program resulted in unnatural offspring termed Nephilim, which derives from the Hebrew naphal (to fall), or the Fallen Ones. The resulting Nephilim apparently also yearned after human women, (the daughters of man) and also took wives with them. According to the Bible, the Nephilim were renowned for both their strength and their wickedness. In return for the human women given to them in marriage, the Nephilim taught mankind many things as described in the Book of Enoch.

The Book of Enoch is an ancient Jewish religious work, traditionally ascribed to Enoch, the great-grandson of Noah. It is not part of the biblical canon as used by Jews, apart from Beta Israel. It is regarded as canonical by the Ethiopian Orthodox Church and the Eritrean Orthodox Church, but no other Christian group.

The older sections of the Book of Enoch which are found mainly in the Book of the Watchers are estimated to date from about 300 BC, and the latest part, found in the Book of Parables, is believed to have been composed at the end of the 1st century BC

A study of such works, however, reveals a great deal of relevant information. For example, the following list is the names of those angelic leaders who descended to take human women as their wives:
- Samayasa, chief among all,
- Urakabrameel,
- Azibeel,
- Tamiel,
- Ramuel,

- Danel,
- Azkeel,
- Sarakuyal,
- Asael,
- Armers,
- Batraal.

According to these ancient texts, these "gods" took wives with whom they had intercourse, to whom also they taught such things as magic, the art of enchantment and the diverse properties of various roots and trees. Amazarac gave instruction in all of the secrets of sorcerers; Barakaial was the master of all of those who study the stars; Akibeel taught the meaning of manifested signs; and Azaradel taught the motions of the moon.

From the reading of the ancient text, such as the Book of Enoch, it would seem that the Nephilim were in full revolt against God himself. Not only had they increased Humanity's knowledge in various areas that God did not want them to know anything about, but they had also tried to sway Man from the true religion of Yahweh.

Figure 14: The Biblical Flood was to cleanse the planet.

In his fury, Yahweh saw that this alliance between subordinate gods and man had caused man to rebel against him just as the B'nai Elohim had done as well, so he decided to cleanse the Earth for all time, Enoch, himself a prophet and a man who had stayed loyal to Yahweh foretold of the judgment of Yahweh and it was his descendant, Noah who built the Ark to preserve the non-polluted human beings from drowning.

However, in spite of Yahweh's intention and rumors to the contrary, the Nephilim were not all destroyed in the flood. In the Book of Numbers 13:33, there appears to be some confusion regarding the word Nephilim as it had probably been translated as simply meaning 'giants' in common with the pre-Olympian Titans. When Joshua's spies reported back from Canaan, they called certain of the inhabitants of Canaan "giants."

"*And there we saw the Nephilim, the sons of Anak, which come of the Nephilim, and we were in our own sight as grasshoppers, and so we were in their sight.*"

However, it is to the explanation of WHO the Nephilim really were that I would like to venture. As will be discussed in another chapter at more length, the Nephilim had a major impact on the human race over the centuries and this impact supports the premise of this work.

Figure 15: Artist's rendition of Zeus, King of the Gods

Hebrew mythology, of which both the B'nai Elohim and Nephilim are part, descended in part from earlier Semitic beliefs. One of the main influences of Hebrew lore is that of the Canaanites. First, let us look at their angelic patriarchs, the B'nai Elohim. As I have said previously the word Elohim is the plural and does not mean God but in fact Gods! Secondly, the god El is the ancient Semitic deity of all things; in fact in myths he is termed bny bnwt, which translates as 'Creator of that which is created'.

Ēl is a Northwest Semitic word meaning "deity". In the Canaanite religion, or Levantine religion as a whole, Ēl or Il was the supreme god, the father of humankind and all creatures and the husband of the goddess Asherah as recorded in the clay tablets of Ugarit.

The noun Ēl was found at the top of a list of gods as the Ancient of gods or the Father of all gods, in the ruins of the royal archive of the Ebla civilization, in the archaeological site of Tell Mardikh in Syria dated to 2300 BC. The bull was symbolic to Ēl and his son Ba'al Hadad, and they both wore bull horns on their headdress. He may have been a desert god at some point, as the myths say that he had two wives and built a sanctuary with them and his new children in the desert. Ēl had fathered many gods, but most important were Hadad, Yam, and Mot.

Figure 16: Symbol of Marduk

He is often portrayed as a king sitting on a throne looking rather aloof and remote. This may be a pictorial representation of the distance and indeed difference that Man has to God (El).

El is also known as the 'Bull' symbolizing both his strength and creative force. He appears to be very much like the Hellenic Kronus and later Zeus, a benevolent patriarchal king. As in most cultures, the ruling King was said to be the 'Servant of El' or indeed son of El.

However, El was comparatively a very young god (only a few thousand years old!) whereas his consort, Elat (Goddess) predated him by many generations. His offspring, the celestial royal family included the following:

Name	Characteristic
Persephone Underworld -	fertility goddess
Athena	War and arts goddess
Eros	God of love (fertility)
Marduck	War, Fertility, Kingship god
Sapas	Solar torch of the gods
Sahar	The Morning Star
Salem	The Evening Star

As one can clearly see, there is a great deal of similarity with that of the better known Hellenic family of Gods, the Olympians and the ancient gods of Canaan. This is probably because the Phoenicians, an off-shoot of the Canaanite people, were great traders and sea-farers; they greatly influenced the ancient Mediterranean world. A good example of this is the similarity of the Semitic alphabet (Aleph, Beth, Gimmel etc.) and the Hellenic one (Alpha, Beta, Gamma etc.) So therefore mythology could be passed on and changed from culture to culture.

In fact, as this is the family of El it would be quite acceptable to label this pantheon as the Elohim - the Many of El. As the culture of Canaan changed, so did the structure of the gods, (Elohim) where Marduk, the young god, replaced El, the old man.

Marduk himself is a changing god; he appears to have been initially a fertility god hence his bull image symbol of procreation and strength. Later on in his career, Marduk became more of a military and state archetype becoming the patron god of Babylon. In this presence it is clear that Marduk, the Biblical Bel (Lord) is chief amongst the Elohim, family of El. Marduk was identified with the Phoenician Baal, a general name given to any local major Semitic deity. The word Baal meaning Lord. In fact the term Baalim means idols or Baals collectively.

Figure 17: Statue to Gilgamesh

Perhaps one of Marduk's greatest feats was the creation of the 'seeds of mankind' with the goddess Aru. Aru appears in many forms and is more commonly known as Ashera, the 'Mother of the Gods'. In fact, she is credited as the mother of Gilgamesh, a very important heroic character from Semitic lore. He, with his companion, Enkidu, travelled throughout the land searching for the home of the gods so that he could become immortal, as befitted the son of a goddess. In the process he was credited with completing many tasks and working numerous miracles. He is very similar to the later Hercules. Gilgamesh is credited with extreme strength and wisdom and like Hercules, was an incarnation of the fertility god.

A link of correspondences can be made between all three myth cycles discussed above. The Canaanite pantheon in this instance begins with El, of course there are other gods before El but that is of no concern at this moment. El is manifested in Greek culture as Kronos and later as Zeus as he became more important to the Hellenic religions. Yahweh is the supreme god of the Hebrew people, but he appears to have borrowed many attributes from many neighboring deities this is probably why he has such a diverse character in the Old Testament.

Figure 18: Many early Kings were said to be sons of the gods.

As head of the royal family, or pantheon, of the Canaanite gods, Baal is the King of the Elohim - Olympians. Beneath this group is the divine spawn of matings with lesser deities, a smaller pantheon, perhaps even the first mating of Gods and Humans, the B'nai Elohim. This breeding may be the condemned (by the Hebrew Rabbis) but the practice of ritual sexual intercourse with High Priest and Priestess is common in many pagan religions. The progeny of these matings would be the Kings and Queens of the land, the earthly incarnation of the divine god(s). The Nephilim themselves seem to be the descendants of these divine terrestrial coupling.

So the mythical Nephilim could be translated as the off-spring of the governing royal body, themselves said to be descended from the Gods. This may be a sound theory but it seems to be too post-Olympian/Elohim and therefore could be a later version of the tale. Yet, all this does not answer why they are called the 'Fallen'. For that I we need to consider that perhaps the Nephilim were actually pre-Olympian. .

If we accept the possibility that ancient aliens may have once roamed this Earth, manipulating the human race and interacting with them, then it may be worth also examining the motivations of these ancient races and how they may coincide with current motivations. If the human element has always been a common factor, then whatever crisis these ancient aliens had at the time has not been solved through technology in the past few thousand years - meaning it may be around a bit longer.

Imagine the apprehension ancient people may have felt seeing creatures from the heavens suddenly landing "sky chariots" in their village and taking people aboard their vessels. Of course it may not have been quite the way it is now. Accounts and pictographs of ancient rituals, now considered apocryphal show people being chosen or sacrificed to these entities. If the rulers were descendants of these space farers, then it is quite possible these ancient beings even used the governments of ancient civilizations to achieve the cooperation or acceptance of their visits.

Of all the paranormal topics discussed in the Bible, the existence of UFOs seems to almost be a given. However, when people think of UFOs, it seems they almost always think of little green (or grey) men with big black eyes who reportedly abduct people at night and perform hideous experiments on them. When I see toys and other items in stores that portray "aliens" or "UFOs" they always seem to picture these same little aliens. However, a reading of the Bible as literature makes it clear that the aliens there were very human looking.

Figure 19: Nordic looking aliens.

If that was all that was out there, I'd have to agree that these little guys don't seem too nice, and they certainly don't seem to be very Biblical. When I first started looking into the whole topic I thought it was very refreshing to find that UFO researchers who are really into this type of stuff generally feel that this type of alien is actually only a small part of the extraterrestrial population. They usually refer to this particular group of aliens as the "Greys."

So why do these Greys get all the publicity? If you think about it, it's really not such a strange concept. Think about other things you see in our society. How many brand names of soda are there in the average grocery store? Probably dozens with many different flavors, but if you just believed what you see on TV, you might think that Coke and Pepsi were the only two soft drinks made. It's kind of the same thing with UFOs and aliens: you could say that the greys just seem to spend more money on advertising.

Figure 20: George Adamski

If there really are other aliens, you might be wondering why these groups don't get much publicity as well. Why are the greys the only ones pictured in all the comic books and TV shows and shown on all the merchandise? Maybe the question we should be asking is *"Where do we go to get the other side of the story?"* During the 1950s and 1960s, it was the tall blonde Nordic looking aliens who seemed to get most of the publicity. George Adamski and Howard Menger wrote a library of books regarding their meetings with these aliens.

If you just look at what's actually in the Bible with an open mind, you can find dozens of UFO accounts. The nice thing about doing this is that it can help you see that there is an alternative to the "Grey" abducting type aliens. People often ask if the aliens are angels or demons as if they can only be one or the other. Isn't it entirely possible - and actually more likely - that they aren't all exactly the same and that some are good and some are bad? Fortunately, all of the Biblical UFOs seem to be working for the good guys.

Now I want to be perfectly clear that I'm not trying to take anything away from the power of God. I'm not saying that God rides a UFO or needs UFOs to perform the miracles attributed to him. But I do think that life exists outside our planet, and I think that God gives these beings the free will choice and opportunity to work with him the same way he gives us the choice to do positive things in our everyday lives.

However, I also believe that early man was led to believe by these alien beings that they were gods in their own rights and they took advantage of early man to the point of holding females in sexual servitude.

CHAPTER FOUR
SECRETS

Now, it is necessary at this point to ask for a certain amount of patience and understanding by the readers. In our examination of secret societies we must first look into the relationship between UFOs and certain ancient secret societies.

Figure 21: UFO seen in Soviet Union

Circumstantially, there is a tremendous body of data that holds that the gods fly in our skies, overseeing their creations. Support for this premise is found in almost every religion in the world.

Among UFO researchers, there is no secret that much information, as well as hard evidence of the reality of the UFO phenomena, has been suppressed both by civilian researchers and by our own Government as well. I am sorry to say that some of the most blatant suppression has actually not been by our Government, but instead as a result of civilian researcher "ego" trips, where one researcher attempts to "own" certain data that should be public domain.

As a result of the suppression and, apparent compartmentalization of other information, the average member of our civilization is, at one and the same time both denied important information and bombarded with conflicting reports of the reality of incidents. Part of our population either does not or will not believe in the existence of possible "little men from outer space". Most point to alleged scientific findings that make such a thing impossible. Other, more inquisitive members of our population, acknowledges the existence of other species or at least the probability of their existence. It is to this part of our population that I direct this book.

An Investigative Nightmare

Investigations into most topics of the paranormal usually results in a tremendous amount of conflicting findings. The research into the UFO mystery seems to follow a similar course. Those who believe that the UFOs are piloted by entities from outer space, tend to find

Figure 22: Cave drawing of alleged giant alien

evidence to support this contention. From eyewitness accounts to landing traces, there is usually so much evidence found to support this contention that it is hard to see where others get the idea that it is all a hoax. However, at the same time, those who do feel that it is all a hoax, can dig around at the alleged landing site and usually find proof that the whole thing was a hoax, usually carried out either by teenagers or publicity seekers, such as the two painters who claim to be responsible for creating every crop circle in the world. Then there is the third group who always feels that a UFO sighting is merely a misidentification of a natural event. There are always claims that they have found some natural happening that could, with a great stretch of the imagination, be mistaken for a landing spaceship. So what are we to believe?

As I have outlined in earlier works, my belief is that we are dealing with a phenomenon that tries to be all things to all people. I believe that it is intentionally misleading researchers in order to protect its' own identity and to limit outside interference in its activities. It takes on many forms in order to deal with many types of people. To those who are fanatically religious, it assumes the cloak of an Angel or a Demon. To those who are prone to believe in life in outer space, it takes on the appearance of a spaceman. But beneath it all, I feel lies an earthbound entity who is fighting for its' own survival. As we progress through this book, I will give my reasons for this belief.

Figure 23: Sky Chariot

In order to deal with the information that I will present and internalize it in such a way that you can begin to understand my theory you will need to suspend your credulity. This subject is so unbelievable that this very fact that it is unbelievable can, and has, acted as a shield for this Entity. For centuries, this force or intelligence, or whatever you want to call it has been leading us down the garden path. It is true, I believe, that this is an Alien Presence, but

I find evidence that it has been here for so long that it is actually more earthling that we are, but more on this point as we go along.

PAWNS OF THE GODS

This Presence has used and abused the human race since before the beginning of recorded history. Whether its' agents pretended to be gods or elves, the Presence has manipulated us all. There is evidence that this Presence has used us as pawns in wars of both attrition and conquest. To it, or them, we are expendable, about as valuable to them as lab rats are to our scientists. As long as what we want corresponds with what it, or they want, everything is fine. In such a case, they are "Benevolent".

It is these "Benevolent Ones" that are making great inroads into the groups of credulous believers. Many such groups spent. And many still spend, one or more evenings a week getting together to study the cosmology of these "Space Brothers". Some have even channeled space brothers and written massive books that have sold well.

Figure 24: George Adamski and his "space brothers"

But let it or their, wants or needs be in conflict with ours and they are not so benevolent. The friendly "Space Brothers" suddenly are not so friendly. We, by that I mean the human race, are somehow necessary to their survival, but only in a general way. Individuals, per se, are not important to them since there are so many humans to choose from. There is also evidence that this entity may have had more than a little to do with our beginnings as a race.

What is upsetting to learn, is that even though this Presence shows no true friendliness toward us, there are actually segments of the human race that have, throughout time, tried to assist this Presence in carrying out its' (or their) mission. From studying ancient records, it would seem that factions of our society have always known of the existence of this Presence, and apparently have been interacting with some of these alleged alien species, who appear to aid the Presence, for quite a while.

Figure 25" Electromagnetic Weapons

The inescapable conclusion is that for centuries beyond measure, humanity has been tricked and betrayed by systems and people set up and led or guided by a Presence with its' own self-interest at heart. Of course, this Presence has not had a free ride; it appears to have an opponent, equally as determined. For this reason, it seems to work through proxies, hence, the existence of secret societies.

In order to achieve what was necessary for its' own good this Presence has used layer upon layer of conspiracies and disinformation to trick and mislead the human race. Using the promise of power, riches and glory, the Presence and its' helpers have converted numerous humans over to its' side. It from these numerous co-opted individuals that the Presence staffs its armies and its secret societies, in order to keep control over the human race.

There is also much evidence that the Presence has been at the bottom of the East West problem. One item of proof, at least circumstantially, is that much of the results of the Russian research into the use of electromagnetic weapons seems to parallel the types of electromagnetically based equipment reportedly used by the Aliens said to come from the UFOs in many of their contacts with humans. Of course, it could be that the Russian researchers just "happened" to stumble across some discoveries in this particular field and it is a coincidence, but it is amazing that their "discoveries" seem to allow them to do the same "miracles" as the flying saucers have been able to do for centuries, such as impossible cures and disabling mechanical devices[16].

Figure 26: Russian Symbol

This area of research will be discussed in a later chapter, but suffice it to say that for any scientific discovery, it should be possible to trace the development of the discovery through a series of earlier related projects. In other words, discoveries do not just spring forth from the alleged discoverer's head, full blown. There should be definable primitive discoveries that lead to ever more

---

[16] Ostrander, Sheila and Lynn Schroeder, Psychic Discoveries Behind the Iron Curtain, Prentice Hall Press, New York. 1970.

complicated discoveries. However in regard to the electromagnetic discoveries of the Russians, in many cases, this is exactly what appears to have happened. In fact, this has happened not only in Russia, but in other countries as well.

You are not being asked to blindly believe what I am about to say, but I do ask that you consider my proposal just as you would a proposal from your investment advisor or your attorney. I am not asking you to invest money in anything, (other than the purchase of this book), but I am asking you to consider what I say. For if I am right, and we act to oppose the Presence, or at least smoke it out, we may have a chance of seeing the next century as a free people. If I am wrong, then we can have a good laugh and no one is hurt. Think of it as flood insurance, you may never need it, but it is better to have it and not need it than to need it and not have it.

ENTERING THE WORLD OF THE STRANGE

I am about to take you into a world that you may not be familiar with. It is a world of ancient legends, and today's headlines, of abductions and mutilations, both human and animal. There will be tales of Secret societies and serious discussions of

Figure 27: Kennedy Assassination

living gods. We will examine abduction reports that have not made the headlines. We will also hear from people who are afraid to come forward under their own names for fear of bodily harm. It is a journey for the strong of heart and mind. Remember, when you read of the experiences of these unfortunate, or fortunate, depending on your point of view, there but for the grace of God, go you.

It may come as a great shock to many, but the UFO research field is complex, confusing and dangerous. It also contains much in the way of valuable truth. Some of the danger comes from the Presence and its' minions. Some of the danger comes from, heretofore unknown, secret societies who serve, perhaps unknowingly, the Presence. Then too, unfortunately, some of the danger comes from our own Government. There have been numerous deaths, accidental and otherwise, among the hard core researchers. Not surprisingly, especially if my theory is correct, those who have died have been those who have seemed to be getting close to something worthwhile in their investigations.

As an aside, in addition to the over twenty witnesses to the actual assassination who died within the first few years after the event, over fifty investigators who have been involved in research that would tend to tie the assassination of John Kennedy with the UFO mystery have met violent deaths[17]. I'm not sure what that means, but it does seem to be something more than coincidence.

Incidentally, as another interesting note, there was an individual making the rounds of the talk shows and speaking on the seminar circuit, who maintained that John Kennedy was killed because he found out the truth about the shadowy organization referred to as MJ 12. In early 1963 President Kennedy was alleged to have given MJ 12 one year in which to reveal the truth to the American Public about the aliens and in addition is alleged to have ordered MJ 12 to stop government involvement in the drug trade.

---

[17] Grodon, Robert J. and Harrison Edward Livingstone, HIGH TREASON, The Conservatory Press. 1989. 469 pages.

As a result, M 12 is supposed to have marked President Kennedy for elimination[18]. This would seem to be an area of investigation perhaps worth following, especially if your life insurance is paid up.

THE GODS CAME DOWN

According to the earliest legends of this planet, found in almost every early civilization on the planet that man was raised by a god, or gods, from his primitive state to become what he (or she) is today. Now comes the question, who were these gods?

Figure 28: Gods of ancient Egypt

According to the Sumerians man was created in the laboratory by the Annunaki[19] to be a worker drone. Either an intention modification or a lab accident gave man the ability to procreate.

Christianity talks about the Hebrew god who created the world in six days and rested on the seventh. Of course even the biblical books seem to have some confusion regarding this concept. God is said to be the one true god, but the word used to describe him in the original

---

[18] Cooper, Milton William, OPERATION MAJORITY, Private printing. Order from Milton William Cooper, 1311 S. Highland #205, Fullerton, CA. 92632.

[19] According to later Babylonian myth, the Annunaki were the children of Anu and Ki, brother and sister gods, themselves the children of Anshar and Kishar (Skypivot and Earthpivot, the Celestial poles), who in turn were the children of Lahamu and Lahmu ("the muddy ones"), names given to the gatekeepers of the Abzu temple at Eridu, the site at which the creation was thought to have occurred. Finally, Lahamu and Lahmu were the children of Tiamat and Abzu.

Hebrew works use the word Elohim. This word is used to refer to the one god and yet Elohim is a Hebrew word which expresses concepts of divinity or deity, notably used as a name of God in Judaism. It is apparently related to the Northwest Semitic word Ēl which means "god". Within the Hebrew language however, Elohim is morphologically a plural, in use both as a true plural with the meaning "angels, gods, rulers" and as a "plural intensive" with singular meaning, referring to a god or goddess, and especially to the single God of Israel .

Figure 29: The late Zacharia Sitchin

But Christianity is not the only religion that uses language that refers to the concept of one God actually being "gods". The ancient Sumerians talk about the creature that came from the sea to teach their remote ancestors the arts of civilization. In the Earth Chronicles series, author Zecharia Sitchin outlined the writings of the ancient Sumerians. According to his translations, the Sumerians believe that they were taught the rudiments of civilization by a being called Oannes.

Oannes was actually the name given by the Babylonian writer Berossa's in the 3rd century BC to a supposedly mythical being who is said to have taught early mankind wisdom. Berossus describes Oannes as having the body of a fish but underneath it was said that he had the figure of a man. This being is described as dwelling beneath the waters of the Persian Gulf. According to the Sumerian writings Oannes rose out of the waters in the daytime and furnished mankind instruction on writing, the arts and the various sciences.

Figure 30: Oannes

The name "Oannes" was once conjectured to be derived from that of the ancient Babylonian god Ea, but it is now known that the name is the Greek form of the Babylonian Uanna (or Uan) a name used for Adapa[20] in

---

[20] Adapa was a mortal from a godly lineage, a son of Ea (Enki in Sumerian, a name specifically applied to one of the leaders of the Annunaki), the god of wisdom and of the ancient city of Eridu, who brought the arts of civilization to that city (from Dilmun, according to some versions). He broke the wings of Ninlil the South Wind, who had overturned his fishing boat, and was called to account before Anu. Ea, his patron god, warned him to apologize humbly for his actions, but not to partake of food or drink while he was in heaven, as it would be the food of death. Anu, impressed by Adapa's sincerity, offered instead the food of immortality, but Adapa heeded Ea's advice, refused, and thus missed the chance for immortality that would have been his.

Adapa is often identified as advisor to the mythical first (antediluvian) king of Eridu, Alulim. In addition to his advisory duties, he served as a priest and exorcist, and upon his death took his place among the Seven Sages or Apkallū. (Apkal, "sage", comes from Sumerian Abgallu (Ab=water, Gal=Great, Lu=man) a reference to Adapa, the first sage's association with water.)

texts from the Library of Ashurbanipal[21]. The Assyrian texts attempt to connect the word to the Akkadian word for a craftsman "ummanu" but this is a merely a pun. Scholars have long speculated that the name might ultimately be derived from that of the 8th century figure of Jonah (Hebrew Yonah). Bible critics have made the reverse claim, although the Hebrew name has the known meaning of "dove". Oannes historically been portrayed as a man wearing the skin of a fish. Or is it perhaps a man, or perhaps Alien, wearing a diving suit? It is a mystery, but some knew the truth.

In fact, each early civilization on this planet talked about a mysterious being that came from nowhere to teach the locals the rudiments of civilization. In each case, once the civilization began to grow in sophistication, the teacher mysteriously vanished into the mists, never to be seen again. Suffice it to say without these mysterious teachers civilization on this planet might be very different.

But now comes some big questions, who were these teachers, where did they come from and where did they go? Of course there is the biggest question of all, were these mysterious teachers who raised the human race from the primitive jungle runners to be civilized actually the gods of antiquity?

In earlier eons, depending on your belief, God, or the gods, dealt directly with man, or at least certain representatives of man. During this same era, God, or one or more of the gods, had relations with human females and

---

[21] Ashurbanipal (Akkadian: Aššur-bāni-apli, "Ashur is creator of an heir"; 685 B.C. – c. 627 B.C.), also spelled Assurbanipal or Ashshurbanipal, was the son of Esarhaddon and the last great king of the Neo-Assyrian Empire (668 B.C. – c. 627 B.C.). He established the first systematically organized library in the ancient Middle East, the Library of Ashurbanipal, which survives in part today at Nineveh. In the Bible he is called Asenappar (Ezra 4:10).[4] Roman historian Justinus identified him as Sardanapalus

gave birth to entities part god and part mortal. These were the famous demi-gods who became the rulers of lesser mortals. These were the sons of the gods. The gods themselves seem to have pulled away from direct contact with man, to oversee things from afar. So what happen?

CHAPTER FIVE
A CLOSER LOOK AT EZEKIAL'S WHEEL

Figure 31: NASA's Logo

Now I think it would be wise to look at one of the most well-known stories of alien contact in the Bible, that of Ezekiel's Wheel. The adventures of Ezekiel are often cited as proof that early man came in contact with unidentified flying objects. The Biblical patriarchs themselves believed that almost everything they saw was a sign from God, but was that just primitive man trying to describe something he had no way to understand or was it something else?

Ezekiel believed that he had seen servants of God when he had his encounter with what has been called Ezekiel's wheel. Since Blumrich\, in his excellent book, has already done an outstanding job in analyzing the reporting in the book of Ezekiel, I'm not going to reinvent the wheel, so to speak, by doing that here. But as an aid to allow the reader to better understand how advanced technology can be mistaken for supernatural events, I am including an analysis of the first chapter of the Book of Ezekiel that is based on the work of NASA Engineer Josef F. Blumrich[22].

The first part of the text shown below is from the Book of Ezekiel[23] and the second part titled Blumrich Summary is a compilation of several documents that discuss Blumrich's beliefs.

Ezekiel 1:4

I looked, and I saw a windstorm coming out of the north--an immense cloud with flashing lightning and surrounded by brilliant light. The center of the fire looked like glowing metal.

Blumrich summary:

Figure 32: Windstorm

The spacecraft appears some distance from the Ezekiel in its initial descent. The vapor cloud that is described as surrounding the metal craft is, in all likelihood from the warmer craft hitting cooler air preliminary to the firing of the propulsion system. The engine is then fired which to a primitive man would look like flashing lightning.

Ezekiel 1:5

And in the fire was what looked like four living creatures. In appearance their form was that of a man

Blumrich summary:

---

[22] Blumrich, Josef F., The Spaceships of Ezekiel, Corgi, 1974.
[23] King James Edition

Keeping in mind that this is a primitive man trying to describe something far advanced beyond anything he has ever seen before, Blumrich believed that the prophet saw four shapes surrounded by fire (engine exhaust perhaps) and vapor that look to hike to be alive. It would appear that these are helicopter-like bodies deployed by the craft before landing.

Ezekiel 1:6
But each of them had four faces and four wings.

Blumrich summary:
The prophet is now able to see more detail because the craft is at a low altitude. Blumrich believed that what Ezekiel saw was the four blades of the rotors and the fairing housings above the rotors that had the appearance of faces.

Ezekiel 1:7
Their legs were straight; their feet were like those of a calf and gleamed like burnished bronze.

Blumrich summary:
Blumrich believes that this is a description of the landing legs which had shock absorbers and round footpads similar in appearance to those of an animal. The example pictured here is not an exact reproduction of the description but it is very similar in regard to the feet which are somewhat rounded

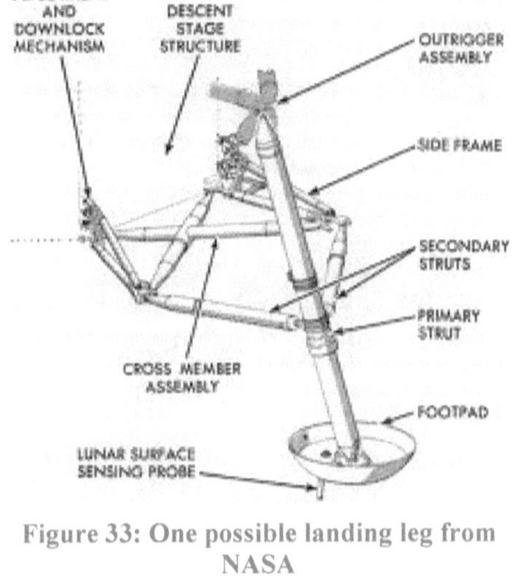

Figure 33: One possible landing leg from NASA

similar to that of a calf.

Ezekiel 1:8

Under their wings on their four sides they had the hands of a man. All four of them had faces and wings,

Blumrich summary:

Many of our exploratory craft have remote control mechanical arms and Blumrich believes that this verse refers to remote-controlled mechanical arms hanging alongside the cylindrical helicopter bodies.

This particular drawing is an artist's rendition of what would fit the description in verses 5 and 8.

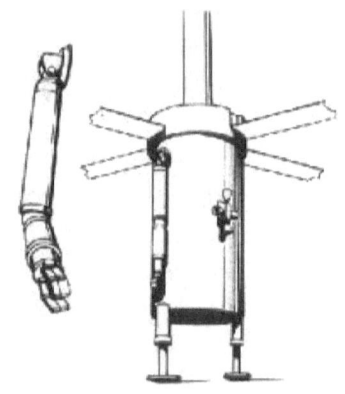

Figure 34: Mechanical arms on a lander.

Ezekiel 1:9

And their wings touched one another. Each one went straight ahead; they did not turn as they moved.

Blumrich summary:

A reference to the helicopter blades protruding outward is made.

Ezekiel 1:10

Their faces looked like this: Each of the four had the face of a man, and on the right side each had the face of a lion, and on the left the face of an ox; each also had the face of an eagle.

Blumrich summary:

The fairing surfaces, which protect the gears and other control devices above the rotors, look to the prophet like faces. The fairings are irregular in shape with some raised and some cut out areas, all of which lends itself to an awe-struck interpretation on the prophet's part. By way of example, Blumrich shows photos of Gemini and Apollo capsules that at certain angles look like monsters. Because like faces face in like directions, we see that the rotors are synchronized at rest position. It should also be pointed out that the fairing could have been designed to look like living creatures for the shock and awe value when the pilots were dealing with the humans.

Ezekiel 1:11
Such were their faces. Their wings were spread out upward; each had two wings, one touching the wing of another creature on either side, and two wings covering its body.

Blumrich summary:
The first part refers to the rotor blades being divided. The suggestion is that there is a kind of gap in the control mechanism or fairing. The last part of the verse refers to the rotor blades folded in an up and down position.

Ezekiel 1:12
Each one went straight ahead. Wherever the spirit would go, they would go, without turning as they went.

Blumrich summary:
This refers to the landing leg assembly and the retractable wheels as part of each leg assembly. Ezekiel doesn't see the wheels until they are actually deployed in verse fifteen. Verses nine, twelve and fifteen are interrelated.

Ezekiel 1:13
The appearance of the living creatures was like burning coals of fire or like torches. Fire moved back and forth among the creatures; it was bright, and lightning flashed out of it.

Blumrich summary:
Ezekiel is referring to the flowing reactor radiator and the bursts from the control rockets. The lightning effect comes from what would seem like leaping random fire but in fact is controlled bursts from the various control rockets for stabilization purposes.

Ezekiel 1:14
The creatures sped back and forth like flashes of lightning.

Blumrich summary:
The spacecraft hovers and moves in various directions until a suitable landing site is found.

Ezekiel 1:15
As I looked at the living creatures, I saw a wheel on the ground beside each creature with its four faces.

Blumrich summary:
The wheels are deployed. They appear at the very moment they become necessary. However, the description of a wheel makes it very clear that Ezekiel was describing something mechanical as he would certainly recognize a wheel, something with which he was quite familiar.

Ezekiel 1:16-21

This was the appearance and structure of the wheels: They sparkled like chrysolite, and all four looked alike. Each appeared to be made like a wheel intersecting a wheel. As they moved, they would go in any one of the four directions the creatures faced; the wheels did not turn about as the creatures went. Their rims were high and awesome, and all four rims were full of eyes all around. When the living creatures moved, the wheels beside them moved; and when the living creatures rose from the ground, the wheels also rose. Wherever the spirit would go, they would go, and the wheels would rise along with them, because the spirit of the living creatures was in the wheels. When the creatures moved, they also moved; when the creatures stood still, they also stood still; and when the creatures rose from the ground, the wheels rose along with them, because the spirit of the living creatures was in the wheels.

Blumrich summary:

The greenish-bluish color of the wheels suggests a protective film or coating. A further description of advanced reversible wheels is given. Ezekiel is confused - looks to him like a wheel within a wheel. These wheels look like they are obeying orders. He has had experience with wheels but these are puzzling. Thus he gives much time to their description. The craft rolls on the ground, probably in a maneuver to find the most suitable site.

Ezekiel 1:22

Spread out above the heads of the living creatures was what looked like an expanse, sparkling like ice, and awesome.

Blumrich summary:

Here is a description of the main body of the craft. We get its basic shape, spreading out like a "firmament." The surface of the main body is metallic, shining, and bright.

Ezekiel 1:23

Under the expanse their wings were stretched out one toward the other, and each had two wings covering its body.

Blumrich summary:

We are given additional information concerning the position of the helicopter-like appendages relative to the main body. Rotor blades are at rest.

Ezekiel 1:24-25

When the creatures moved, I heard the sound of their wings, like the roar of rushing waters, like the voice of the Almighty, like the tumult of an army. When they stood still, they lowered their wings. Then there came a voice from above the expanse over their heads as they stood with lowered wings.

Blumrich summary:

Blumrich feels these verses are out of order. They describe operating rotor blade motors and the resultant sound effects.

Ezekiel 1:26

Above the expanse over their heads was what looked like a throne of sapphire, and high above on the throne was a figure like that of a man.

Blumrich summary:

The prophet sees the command module shaped and colored like a cabochon-cut sapphire. Seated in the pilot's seat is a man.

Ezekiel 1:27

I saw that from what appeared to be his waist up he looked like glowing metal, as if full of fire, and that from there down he looked like fire; and brilliant light surrounded him.

Blumrich summary:

The prophet describes the light effects of the commander's flight suit which, in Blumrich's opinion, are reminiscent of the light effects caused by the reflecting surfaces of certain insulation materials used in the Apollo lunar module. (See Rev 1:12-15 and Dan 10:6)

It might be enlightening here to mention the light effects, especially the golden glow effect, described by some present-day witnesses to UFO close encounters, people who have been in near proximity to UFO crew members. A classic example of such an effect would be the Fatima incident earlier in the century. An interesting explanation of this effect is offered by an extraterrestrial in Charles Silva's "Date With The Gods."

Ezekiel 1:28

Like the appearance of a rainbow in the clouds on a rainy day, so was the radiance around him. This was the appearance of the likeness of the glory of the LORD. When I saw it, I fell facedown, and I heard the voice of one speaking.

Blumrich summary:

Here are the optical light effects of the translucent cabochon-shaped command module sitting atop the main body of the spacecraft. Sunlight hitting the translucent surface and reflecting off other surfaces inside the module causes a rainbow light effect. (See Enoch 14:9-22 and Rev 4:3) Blumrich emphasizes that the brightness was "round about him." It did not emanate from "him." Him, we should carefully note, refers to Ezekiel's initial mistake of identity - confusing the spacecraft with God himself.

CHAPTER SIX
MEN FROM THE SHADOWS

As outlined previously, it is the belief of this author that there exists a well-organized group of individuals, or, if you prefer, entities, that openly ruled this world at the beginning of time and now continues to control activities on the planet from behind the scenes. A portion of this control is exercised through manipulation of our beliefs in the supernatural and the paranormal. However, to begin to see the true picture there is a great deal of misdirection that must be gotten through first.

THE ANNUNAKI

There are many legends that hold that the original visitors to this planet, those our ancestors would eventually call gods were a race referred to at the dawn of history as

Figure 35: From Summerian culture, the Annunaki.

the Annunaki. However, historically the Annunaki (also variously referred to as: Anunna, Anunnaku, Ananaki and a number of other variations) are best known as a group of Sumerian, Akkadian and Babylonian deities. The name is variously written "da-nuna", "da-nuna-ke4-ne", or "da-nun-na", meaning something to the effect of 'those of royal blood' or 'princely offspring'.

There was another race that our ancestors look at as gods that were referred to as the Igigi. The Annunaki relation to the Igigi[24] is unclear - at times the names are used synonymously but in the Atra-hasis flood myth the Igigi were actually part of the Annunaki only they were assigned to duty in space to overlook the planet. However, the legends also say that they rebelled after 40 days and were replaced by the creation of the human race.

Jeremy Black and Anthony Green[25] offer a slightly different perspective on the Igigi and the Annunaki, writing that "Igigu or Igigi is a term introduced in the Old Babylonian Period as a name for the (ten) 'great gods'.

While it sometimes kept that sense in later periods, from Middle Babylonian times on it is generally used to refer to the gods of heaven collectively, just as the term Anunnakku (Anuna) was later used to refer to the gods of the underworld. In the Epic of Creation, it is said that there are 300 Igigu of heaven[26]." These 300 hundred were said to be those who looked down from above or the Watchers.

---

[24]Igigi is a term that is used to refer to the gods of heaven in Sumerian mythology

[25]Black, Jeremy and Anthony Green, Gods, demons and symbols of ancient Mesopotamia: an illustrated dictionary. London: British Museum Press, 1992.

[26]These gods of heaven are also related to the "Watchers."

These early gods, called the Anunnaki, appear in the Babylonian creation myth, *Enuma Elish*. In the later version of this myth, magnifying the great god Marduk, after the creation of mankind, Marduk divides the Anunnaki and assigns them to their proper stations, three hundred in heaven, three hundred on the earth. In gratitude, the Anunnaki, the "Great Gods", built Esagila, the splendid: "*They raised high the head of Esagila equaling Apsu. Having built a stage-tower as high as Apsu, they set up in it an abode for Marduk, Enlil, and Ea.*" Then they built their own shrines.

Figure 36: Winged Bull

According to later Babylonian myths, the Anunnaki were the children of Anu and Ki, brother and sister gods, themselves the children of Anshar and Kishar (Skypivot and Earthpivot, the Celestial poles), who in turn were the children of Lahamu and Lahmu ("the muddy ones"), names given to the gatekeepers of the Abzu temple at Eridu, the site at which the creation was thought to have occurred. Finally, Lahamu and Lahmu were the children of Tiamat and Abzu two of the earliest and most senior gods.

THE MYSTERIOUS ROBED ONES

In addition to the Annunaki, there were also the mysterious teachers who spread the gift of knowledge to many of the primitive cultures on this planet. There have also been numerous other stories about individuals wearing blacked hooded robes that have appeared at various times in our history to sort of nudge history in the direction that they wanted it to go.

As one example there was Johann Friedrich Schweitzer[27], also known as Joannes Fridericus Helvetius, in Latin, often known simply as Helvetius the grandfather of the celebrated philosopher of the same name. He was an alchemist who labored ceaselessly to fathom the mystery of the "philosopher's stone," the legendary catalyst that would allow him to transmute base metals into gold.

According to a story handed down through history, one day in 1666 when he was working in his laboratory at the Hague, a stranger attired all in black, as befitted a respectable burgher of North Holland, appeared and informed him that he would remove all the alchemist's doubts about the existence of the philosopher's stone[28], for he himself possessed such an object.

Figure 37: Robed figure

---

[27] Johann Friedrich Schweitzer (1625–1709) was a Dutch physician and alchemical writer, of German extraction. He is known for his book Vitulus Aureus (The Golden Calf), published in 1667. Another book is Ichts aus Nichts, für alle Begierigen der Natur from 1655. He is notorious for the story that he actually carried out transmutation of lead into gold. He is also said to have been physician to the Prince of Orange of the time. His birthplace is given as Köthen, He was an ancestor of the philosopher Claude-Adrien Helvétius

[28] The philosopher's stone is a legendary alchemical substance said to be capable of turning base metals (lead, for example) into gold (chrysopoeia) or silver. It was also sometimes believed to be an elixir of life, useful for rejuvenation and possibly for achieving immortality. For many centuries, it was the most sought-after goal in Western alchemy. The philosopher's stone was the central symbol of the mystical terminology of alchemy, symbolizing perfection at its finest,

The stranger immediately drew from his pocket a small ivory box, containing three pieces of metal the color of brimstone. With those three bits of metal, he said, he could make as much as twenty tons of gold.

The alchemist examined the pieces of metal and seeing that they were very brittle, he surreptitiously scraped off a small portion with his thumbnail. He then returned the three pieces of metal to his mysterious visitor and invited him to perform the process of transmutation. The stranger answered that he was not allowed to do so. It was enough that he had verified the existence of the metal to Helvetius. It was his purpose only to offer him encouragement in his experiments.

After the man's departure, Helvetius procured a crucible and a portion of lead, into which, when in a state of fusion, he threw the stolen grain he had secretly scraped from the alleged philosopher's stone. He was disappointed to find that the grain evaporated, leaving the lead in its original state. Thinking that he had been made a fool by the mad burgher's whimsy, Helvetius returned to his own experiments in attaining the philosopher's stone.

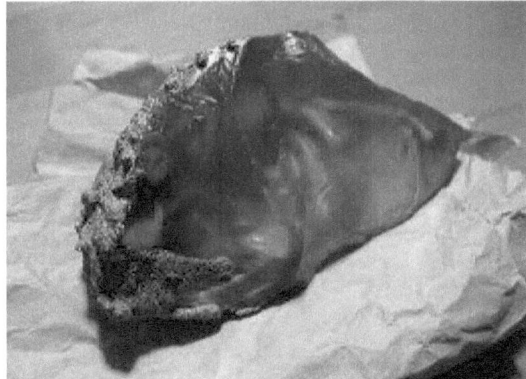

Figure 38: Philosopher's Stone

---

enlightenment, and heavenly bliss. Efforts to discover the philosopher's stone were known as the Magnum Opus.

Some weeks later, when he had almost forgotten the incident, Helvetius received another visit from the stranger. Impatiently, the alchemist told the man that if he could not do as he claimed, then please leave the laboratory at once.

"Very well," the stranger said, consenting to perform a demonstration of the philosopher's stone for the skeptical Helvetius. "I shall show you that that which you most desire does truly exist."

Figure 39: The Alchemist at work.

The mysterious visitor said that one grain was sufficient, but it was necessary to envelope it in a ball of wax before throwing it on the molten metal; otherwise, its extreme volatility would cause it to vaporize.

To Helvetius's astonishment, the stranger transmuted several ounces of lead into gold. Then he permitted the alchemist to repeat the experiment by himself, and Helvetius converted six ounces of lead into very pure gold.

Helvetius found it impossible to keep a secret of such immense value and importance. Soon the word of the alchemist's remarkably successful experiments spread all over The Hague, and Helvetius demonstrated the power of the philosopher's stone in the presence of the Prince of Orange, and many times afterward, until he had exhausted the supply of catalytic pieces that he received from the mysterious burgher.

And search as he might, Helvetius could not find the man in all of North Holland nor learn his name. And pray as he might, the stranger never again visited Helvetius in his study. All that Helvetius was left with was the knowledge that the philosopher's stone was real.

Down through the centuries, very mysterious individuals have appeared at certain moments in human history and provided convincing demonstrations that "impossible" inventions are possible.

The "respectable burgher of North Holland" had appeared "modest and simple" to the alchemist Helvetius. It was his incredible scientific knowledge that startled and inspired the alchemists of Helvetius's day, and though these learned and determined men never did acquire the philosopher's stone that would transmute lead into gold, they did fashion the seeds of the science of chemistry that has accomplished so many transmutations of the human environment and the human condition in the last three hundred years.

While most people look at alchemy as bunk, in fact it was the study of alchemy that gave rise to many of the great scientific advances in history. It was out of the smoky laboratories of the alchemists that:

- Albert le Grand produced potassium lye

- Raymond Lully prepared bicarbonate of potassium

- Paracelsus described zinc and introduced chemical compounds in medicine

- Blaise Vigenere discovered benzoic acid

- Basil Valentine perfected sulfuric acid

- Johann Friedrich Boetticher became the first European to produce porcelain

While each of the above is an important discovery, there are rumors that lying amidst the musty pages of certain ancient alchemical laboratories there are recorded experiments with photography, radio transmission, phonography, aerial flight and numerous other areas of research.

Throughout the Middle Ages and the Renaissance, there were many scholars who claimed that they had received late-night visits from mysterious members of an unnamed secret society that had accomplished the transmutation of metals, the means of prolonging life, the knowledge to see and to hear what was occurring in distant places, and the ability to travel across the heavens in heavier-than-air vehicles.

Some students of the history of alchemy have stated that crumbling, yellowed records of the stupendous achievements of so called alchemists remain hidden in dusty libraries all over the world - more than 100,000 ancient volumes written in a code that has never been sufficiently deciphered.

Numerous occult groups have been created around the belief that centuries ago a secret society achieved a very high level of scientific knowledge that they carefully guarded from the rest of humanity. According to these occultists, certain men of genius in ancient Egypt and Persia were given access to the records of the advanced technologies of the antediluvian world of Atlantis. Many hundreds of years ago, these ancient masters learned to duplicate many of the feats of the Titans of the lost continent.

Figure 40: There are many legends of a mysterious elder race.

There are persistent legends in nearly every culture that tell of an Elder Race that populated the Earth millions of years ago. The Old Ones, who may originally have been of extraterrestrial origin, were an immensely intelligent and scientifically advanced species who eventually chose to structure their own environment under the surface of the planet's soil and seas.

According to legend, the Old Ones usually remain aloof from the surface dwellers, but from time to time throughout history, usually at pivotal point in time, they have been known to visit certain of Earth's more intelligent members in the guise of alchemists or mysterious scientists in order to offer constructive criticism and, in some cases, to give valuable advice in the material sciences.

The Buddhists have incorporated Agharta, an ancient subterranean empire, into their theology and fervently believe in its existence and in the reality of underworld supermen who periodically surface to oversee the progress of the human race. According to one source, the underground kingdom of Agharta was created when the ancestors of the present day cave dwellers drove the Serpent People from the caverns during an ancient war between the reptilian humanoids and the ancient human society.

The decision to form an ancient secret society may have been based on the members' highly developed moral sense and their recognition of the awesome position of responsibility that the discovery of such applications of ancient knowledge had placed upon them. They may have decided to keep their own counsel until the rest of the world had become enlightened enough to deal wisely with such a high degree of technical accomplishments.

From time to time, the secret society may decide the time is propitious to make one of its discoveries known to the "outside world." Such intervention in the affairs of humankind is usually accomplished by carefully feeding certain fragments of research to "outside" scientists whose work and attitude have been judged particularly deserving. When these scientists accomplish the breakthroughs in their research, they credit the success of the experiments to their own diligence, and the secrecy the society prizes so highly is maintained.

On the other hand, the secret society may feel little or no responsibility of any kind to those humans outside of their group. They may be merely biding their time until they turn the great mass of humanity into their slaves.

By the 1840s, the legend of Agharta had already been widely circulated among the mystically minded in Germany. According to this ancient tradition, the Master of the World already controlled many of the kings and rulers of the surface world by exercising his occult powers. Soon this Master and his super race would launch an invasion of Earth and subjugate all humans to his will.

If certain master magicians, disciples of the Titans, individuals of exceptional intellect, power, and wealth, actually did achieve a high degree of technical accomplishment several centuries ago, then they could very well be responsible for a good many of the strange and mysterious vehicles seen in our skies. And if alien life-forms apprehended their advanced technology at the end of the previous century, then they might have established an alliance with the society of humans that easily appeared to be the more advanced and worthy to receive the benefits of their extraterrestrial super-science.

THE MYSTERIOUS AIRSHIP

The year 1897 may have seemed an ideal time to show the "outsiders" just how far advanced the members of the ancient secret society really were. The science of the outsiders seemed as though it had gone about as far as it could go, and it was poised confidently on the brink of the twentieth century.

Interestingly enough many of these new advancements were publically "discovered" by some of the world's most learned men and women who were filled with pride over a host of new technological accomplishments. Of course in the mind of this author, the question is whether these "learned men" were really the originator of these advancements or whether they were guided.

Figure 41: Side view of the mysterious airship.

As an example of some of the advances that took place at this time frame:

- In 1893, Karl Benz and Henry Ford built their first four-wheeled automobiles;

- In 1889 Thomas Edison's Kinetoscope was among the first practical systems of cinematography;

- In 1895, Louis and Auguste Lumiere presented the first commercial projection;

- In that same year, Wilhelm Roentgen discovered X rays, Marconi invented radio telegraphy, and

Konstantin Tsiolkovsky formulated the principle of rocket reaction propulsion;

- In 1896, William Ramsay isolated helium, Ernest Rutherford accomplished the magnetic detection of electrical waves, and Henri Becquerel discovered radioactivity;
- The Royal Automobile Club was founded in London in 1897, and cars were going faster every year;

Figure 42: Similar to the mystery airship

However, with all of these scientific marvels about which to boast, there were as yet no heavier-than-air aerial vehicles to occupy the efforts and the interests of potential aviators; and a good number of brilliant scientists of great reputation had gone on record with their arguments that it was aerodynamically impossible to build such a flying machine.

On the other hand, the future of balloon transport seemed promising, and gondolas could be attached to carry passengers. With all the other wonders of modern science, how could anyone bemoan the lack of heavier-than-air flying machines?

And yet, in March of 1897, a bizarre aircraft, often described as resembling a cone-shaped steamboat, was seen flying across the United States and later throughout the world.

Figure 43: Artist rendition of 1897 mystery airship.

The German Count Ferdinand von Zeppelin did not build his famous airship, a rigid dirigible, until 1898.

Could some mysterious unknown inventors have beaten Count von Zeppelin to the drawing board with a much more impressive vehicle, a forerunner of the modern passenger plane? Or was a secret terrestrial society of master magicians once again displaying their superiority over the outsiders?

The flights of the enigmatic airship continued until August of 1897 when the craft was sighted off the coast of Norway and over Vancouver, British Columbia on the same day.

After a twelve-year absence, the airship reappeared over England in 1909. Within a matter of days, it was sighted over New Zealand, Arkansas, Massachusetts, Rhode Island, West Virginia, and Tennessee. Its final appearance seems to have been over Memphis on January 20, 1910.

Figure 44: Symbol of the Vril Society

In 1871, occultist Edward Bulwer-Lytton wrote *The Coming Race*[29], a novel about a small group of German mystics who had discovered a race of supermen living within the Earth's interior. The super race had built a paradise based on The Vril Force, a form of energy so powerful that the older beings had outlawed its use as a potential weapon. The Vril was believed to have been derived from the Black Sun, a large ball of "Prima Materia" that provided light and radiation to the inhabitants of the inner Earth. It is these

Figure 45: Symbol of the Black Sun

---

[29]Bulwer-Lytton, Edward, The Coming Race, 1871

same inner earth inhabitants that are believed by many to be the makers and pilots of the unidentified flying objects.

In 1919, Karl Haushofer[30] founded the Brothers of the Light Society in Berlin, and soon changed its name to the Vril Society. As Haushofer's Vril Society grew in prominence, it united three major occult societies, the Lords of the Black Stone, the Black Knights of the Thule Society, and the Black Sun and chose the swastika, the hooked cross, as its symbol of the worship of the Black Sun. As with many secret groups, there appears to have been more than one order - those who followed the Golden Sun and those who followed the Black Sun.

Figure 46: Karl Haushofer and Rudolf Hess

The Black Sun, like the Swastika, is a very ancient symbol. While the Swastika represents the eternal fountain of creation, the Black Sun is even older, suggesting the very void of creation itself. The symbol on the Nazi flag is the Thule Sonnenrad (Sun Wheel), not a reversed good luck

---

[30] Karl Ernst Haushofer (August 27, 1869 – March 10, 1946) was a German general, geographer and geopolitician. Through his student Rudolf Hess, Haushofer's ideas may have influenced the development of Adolf Hitler's expansionist strategies, although Haushofer denied direct influence on the Nazi regime. Under the Nuremberg Laws, Haushofer's wife and children were categorized as mischlinge. His son, Albrecht, was issued a German Blood Certificate through the help of Hess.

Swastika. The Black Sun can be seen in many ancient Babylonian and Assyrian places of worship.

While these societies borrowed some concepts and rites from various Hermetic groups, they placed special emphasis on the innate mystical powers of the Aryan race. The Vril and its fellow societies maintained that the Germanic/Nordic/Teutonic people were of Aryan origin, and that Christianity had destroyed the power of the Teutonic civilization in its rise to power.

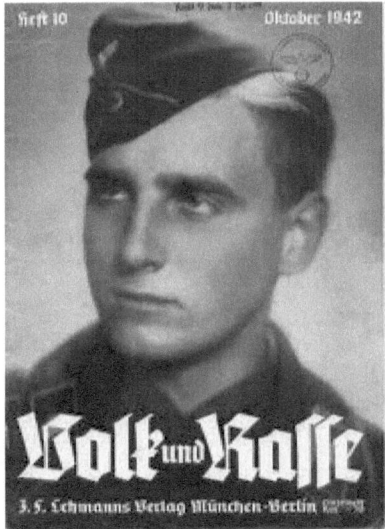

Figure 47: The so-called model for the master race.

The secret societies formed in Germany wanted desperately to prove themselves worthy of working with the super humans that they were positive lived beneath the surface of the planet and they wished to be able to control the incredibly powerful Vril force which would make them the master of the planet.

This ancient force was not unknown, in fact it had been known among the alchemists and magicians as:

- Chi
- Odic force
- Orgone

- Astral Light...

No matter what this force was called, those that worked with it were well aware of its transformative powers to create supermen of ordinary mortals.

The Vril Lodge believed that those who learned control of the Vril would become master of themselves, those around them, and the world itself, if they should so choose. In other words, use of this force could give one the power to rule the world. This ability was of great interest to some members of the Lodge such as Adolf Hitler, Heinrich Himmler, Hermann Goring, and Dr. Theodor Morell, Hitler's personal physician as well as a number of other top Nazi leaders.

Figure 48: It is said that under the Vril guidance the Nazis built a saucer craft.

In fact the Nazi leadership became obsessed with preparing German youth to become a Master Race so the Lords of the Inner Earth would find them worthy above all others when they emerged from their hidden cities to evaluate the people of Earth's nations. There are many who believe that the Lords of the Inner Earth are the descendants of those who first colonized the earth from space.

In 1921, Maria Orsic (Orsitch), a medium in the Vril Society, which had now been renamed Vril Gesellschaft, began claiming that he was receiving spirit messages that were originating from Aryan aliens on Alpha Centauri in the Aldeberan star system. Through these channeled messages Orsitch and another medium that by the name of Sigrun, learned that the aliens spoke of two classes of people on their world, the Aryan, or master race and a subservient planetary race that had evolved through mutation and climate changes

Figure 49: Symbol of the Thule Society.

According to the channeled messages, a half billion years ago, the Aryans, also known as the Elohim[31] or Elder Race, began to colonize our solar system. On the planet Earth, the Aryans were identified as the Sumerians until they elected to carve out an empire for themselves in the hollow of the planet.

Students of the Vril Society also insist that extraterrestrials worked with Nazi scientists to create early models of flying saucers. According to some researchers, an alien tutor race secretly began cooperating with certain German scientists from the Thule, the Vril, and the Black Sun societies in the late 1920s. Working in underground bases with the alien intelligences, the Nazis mastered

---

[31] An ancient Hebrew term for gods.

antigravity space flight, established space stations, accomplished time travel, an developed their spacecraft to warp speeds.

In 1922, members of Thule and Vril claim to have built the Jenseitsflugmaschine, the Other World Flight Machine, based on the psychic messages received from the Aldeberan aliens. W. O. Schulmann of the Technical University of Munich was in charge of the project until it was halted in 1924, and the craft was stored in Messerschmitt's Augsburg. In 1937, after Hitler came into power, he authorized the construction of the Rund flugzeug, the round, or disk-shaped vehicle, for military use and for spaceflight.

Figure 50: Nazi radar facility Isle of Rugen.

In April, 1942, Nazi Germany sent out an expedition composed of a number of its most visionary scientists to seek a military vantage point in the hollow earth. Although the expedition of leading scientists left at a time when the Third Reich was putting maximum effort in their drive against the Allies, Goering, Himmler, and Hitler are said to have enthusiastically endorsed the project. Steeped in the more esoteric teachings of metaphysics, the Fuehrer had long been convinced that

Earth was concave and that a master race lived on the inside of the planet.

The Nazi scientists who left for the island of Rugen had complete confidence in the validity of their quest to find an entrance to the inner world. In their minds, such a coup as discovering the opening to the Inner World would not only provide them with a military advantage, but it would go a long way in convincing the Masters who lived there that the German people truly deserved to mix their blood with them in the creation of a hybrid master race to occupy the surface world, truly a New World Order.

In 1991 when President George H.W. Bush began speaking about a New World Order to beef up his campaign for reelection, evangelist Pat Robertson, who was briefly a presidential candidate, passionately spoke out that "new world order" was actually a code for a secret group that sought to replace Christian society with a worldwide atheistic socialist dictatorship. In his view, and that of many others, there was a group working behind the scenes to bring about this dictatorship.

Figure 51: One symbol of the New World Order

Bush, the conspiracy buffs charged, was a member of one of the world's most devilish and powerful secret societies: the Order of Skull and Bones. What was more,

Figure 52: Symbol of the Council on Foreign Relations

according to these same conspiracists, Bush was also linked to the Bilderbergers, the Council on Foreign Relations (CFR) and the Trilateral Commission, dangerous elitist organizations. It was also pointed out that the CFR was organized by the British Round Table Group which in turn was funded by a bequest from the Last Will and Testament of Cecil Rhodes. The purpose of this bequest was to keep the British Empire the most powerful country in the world.

At about the same time that President Bush's alleged secret affiliations were being exposed, a number of fundamentalist evangelists began to take their first real notice of the UFO phenomenon and saw the mysterious aerial objects as the "signs in the skies" referred to in apocalyptic literature and in the book of Revelation.

It was a short leap for many evangelists to begin to blend accounts of UFOs with the secret societies of top U.S. government officials, politicians, corporate chairmen, international bankers, and many others who sought to bring into being the dreaded "New World

Figure 53: Trilateral Commission

Order."

According to the proponents of this cosmic conspiracy, when President Ronald Reagan gave his famous "alien invasion" speech to the entire United Nations General Assembly in September of 1987, he had already secretly advised representatives of the 176 member nations that the leaders of their respective governments must meet the demands of the technologically superior extraterrestrials or be destroyed.

As Reagan said in his speech:

"I occasionally think how quickly our differences worldwide would vanish if we were facing an alien threat from outside this world. And yet I ask you, is not an alien threat already among us?"

Some UFO researchers have warned that highly placed members of an ancient secret society that can trace its origins beyond the temples of ancient Egypt to Atlantis have established a plan to create a carefully staged "alien invasion" that will convince the masses of the world that a real-life War of the Worlds alien attack is about to begin. People of all nations will believe their leaders who say that

Figure 54: Alien Invasion.

it has been learned that the aliens are a benevolent species and that unconditional surrender to them is for everyone's own good. Immediately following the "surrender" to the aliens, the leaders of the ancient secret society will form a One World Government, a New World Order, thus fulfilling biblical prophecies about a return to the days of Babylon.

Concern over interference by secret societies in the affairs of government was considered very real long before our present-day paranoia. For hundreds of years, certain scholars have worried about global conspiracies being conducted in secret by such groups as the Knights Templar, the Vril, the Thule, the Black Sun, and the Illuminati - who may all be waiting until the propitious time to complete world domination.

Figure 55: Benjamin Disraeli

In 1876, Benjamin Disraeli, British prime minister, warned:

"The governments of the present day have to deal not merely with other governments, with emperors, kings, and ministers, but also with the secret societies which have everywhere their unscrupulous agents, and can at the last moment upset all the governments' plans."

Even those at the highest of the levels of power are well aware that there are forces operating behind the scenes that exercise tremendous power.

CHAPTER SEVEN
OTHER INSTANCES OF ALIEN INVOLVEMENT

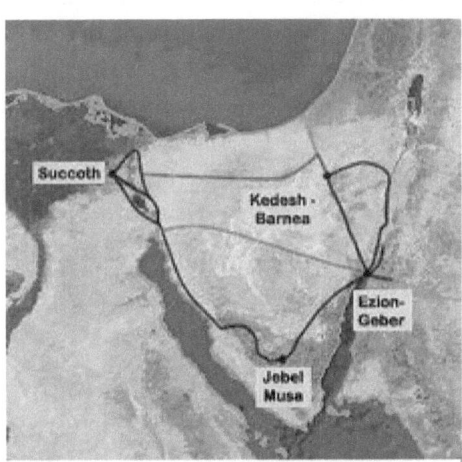

Figure 56: Path the Hebrews followed on the Exodus from Egypt

The Book of Exodus or, simply, Exodus, is the second book of the Hebrew Bible, and of the five books of the Torah (the Pentateuch). The Greek and English name originates with the Septuagint translation of the 3rd century BCE

The book tells how the children of Israel leave slavery in Egypt through the strength of Yahweh, the God who has chosen Israel as his people. Led by their prophet Moses they journey through the wilderness to Mount Sinai, where Yahweh promises them the land of Canaan (the "Promised Land") in return for their faithfulness. The national of Israel enters into a covenant with Yahweh who gives them their laws and instructions for the Tabernacle, the means by which he will dwell with them and lead them to the land.

Traditionally ascribed to Moses himself, modern scholarship sees the book as initially a product of the Babylonian exile (6th century BCE), with final revisions in the Persian post-exilic period (5th century).

When Moses led the Israelites out of slavery in Egypt he certainly didn't do it alone. From the account recorded in the book of Exodus, it seems he had a lot of help from above, and this help appeared in a very unordinary way.

Now remember that when the history of that journey was recorded, the author of the story of Exodus didn't have modern words like "UFO" or even "airplane" to describe what was witnessed by the Hebrews. Think about it, how would you describe a UFO if you couldn't use any modern words? I'd imagine you'd compare it to something that people would be familiar with such as a pillar of fire or a cloud. Even today people refer to "cigar shaped" or "saucer shaped" UFOs as a sort of verbal shorthand.

With this in mind, let's look at the first account of the strange object that appeared to lead the Israelites shortly after they left Egypt:

Exodus 13: 21-22

By day the LORD went ahead of them in a pillar of cloud to guide them on their way and by night in a pillar of fire to give them light, so that they could travel by day or night. Neither

Figure 57: Pillar of fire

the pillar of cloud by day nor the pillar of fire by night left its place in front of the people.

The object is described as a "pillar" - certainly a common visual picture for anyone who lived during that time. But what would we think today if we saw this object that is compared to a pillar of cloud and fire?

Looking at the event from today's perspective, the would not be much question in my mind that a large object like this that could move on its own would likely be some type of aerial vehicle. Given the lack of roads, this vehicle probably would have had to travel off the ground - either hovering or flying - to be this mobile.

Figure 58: Depiction of the Angel of God

It's interesting how the same object is described as a "cloud" during the day - you'll see this visualization used later in the story too. I would suspect that the craft was using the cloud during the day cover its appearance from the Hebrews and lights at night when the lights themselves would make their appearance. As far as describing the object as a pillar of fire at night, how else would you describe an object that was illuminated if you weren't familiar with electric lights?

The following event gives further evidence that this pillar was much more than just your average cloud:

Exodus 14: 19-20

Then the angel of God, who had been traveling in front of Israel's army, withdrew and went behind them. The pillar of cloud also moved from in front and stood behind them, coming between the armies of Egypt and Israel. Throughout the night the cloud brought darkness to the one side and light to the other side; so neither went near the other all night long.

It seems this object was very mobile and it also seemed to be under some kind of intelligent control. I also wonder what the "angel of God" that is mentioned looked like. Do you think it might have been another smaller UFO? From what is recorded in the Exodus account we don't really know for sure, but the description of its movements would make this a reasonable possibility.

This also raises another interesting question. If there was an all-powerful ethereal God behind the Exodus why not immediately move the people in a twinkling of an eye? Why did the Angel of Lord have to be ready to defend the Hebrews from the Army of Pharaoh? Seems rather like an intervention in human affairs by a force from an advanced culture.

Parting the Red Sea

Now if you are open to the possibility that an aerial craft was assigned to assist Moses as he led the Israelites out of Egypt, do you think it might have had something to do with the parting of the Red Sea?

Exodus 14: 21-29

Then Moses stretched out his hand over the sea, and all that night the LORD drove the sea back with a strong east wind and turned it into dry land. The waters were divided, and the Israelites went through the sea on dry ground, with a wall of water on their right and on their left.

Figure 59: Parting of the Red Sea

The Egyptians pursued them, and all Pharaoh's horses and chariots and horsemen followed them into the sea. During the last watch of the night the LORD looked down from the pillar of fire and cloud at the Egyptian army and threw it into confusion.

He made the wheels of their chariots come off so that they had difficulty driving. And the Egyptians said, "Let's get away from the Israelites! The LORD is fighting for them against Egypt."

Then the LORD said to Moses, "Stretch out your hand over the sea so that the waters may flow back over the Egyptians and their chariots and horsemen."

Moses stretched out his hand over the sea, and at daybreak the sea went back to its place. The Egyptians were fleeing toward it, and the LORD swept them into the sea. The water flowed back and covered the chariots and

Figure 60: Egyptian War Chariot

horsemen--the entire army of Pharaoh that had followed the Israelites into the sea. Not one of them survived.

But the Israelites went through the sea on dry ground, with a wall of water on their right and on their left.

When an author talked about this on my radio show[32], I had a number of listeners ask the same question.

"If the UFO was doing all the work, why did Moses have to extend his arms? Why didn't the craft simply fly over the Hebrews and part the waters instead of making it look like Moses was working a miracle?"

Remember that if this object was a UFO, it was there to do the will of God. Since Moses was God's chosen representative to lead the people, the UFO was probably focused on providing technical backup for Moses, not to steal the show. Besides it was more dramatic for a man to work such a miracle and show the power of God than for a mechanical device such as a craft to arrive and demonstrate its power. In fact, this is exactly what Moses is told in a later passage:

Exodus 19: 9

The LORD said to Moses, "I am going to come to

you in a dense cloud, so that the people will hear me speaking with you and will always put their trust in you."

This really does not make a great deal of sense. Today it would

---

[32] The Ken Hudnall Show heard on http://www.borderlandradio.com – Monday through Friday from 8:00 PM Eastern time until 11:00 PM Eastern time.

have religious leaders screaming witchcraft. However, a pillar of cloud would make sense if you were trying to hide your vehicle.

In a later account, the cloud is again involved in a miracle. As in the case of the parting of the Red Sea, it would seem that this cloud covered vehicle had many varied abilities and also furnished food and other things needed by the Hebrews.

Exodus 16: 10-15

While Aaron was speaking to the whole Israelite community, they looked toward the desert, and there was the glory of the LORD appearing in the cloud.

The LORD said to Moses, "I have heard the grumbling of the Israelites. Tell them, 'At twilight you will eat meat, and in the morning you will be filled with bread. Then you will know that I am the LORD your God.' "

That evening quail came and covered the camp, and in the morning there was a layer of dew around the camp. When the dew was gone, thin flakes like frost on the ground appeared on the desert floor. When the Israelites saw it, they said to each other, "What is it?" For they did not know what it was. Moses said to them, "It is the bread the LORD has given you to eat." We've referred to it as Manna.

More References to the Cloud

As the journey goes on, there are a number of other references to God appearing in a cloud or using a cloud to perform certain tasks:

Exodus 19:16-22 (NIV)

On the morning of the third day there was thunder and lightning, with a thick cloud over the mountain, and a very loud trumpet blast. Everyone in the camp trembled.
Then Moses led the people out of the camp to meet with God, and they stood at the foot of the mountain. Mount

Sinai was covered with smoke, because the LORD descended on it in fire. The smoke billowed up from it like smoke from a furnace, the whole mountain trembled violently, and the sound of the trumpet grew louder and louder. Then Moses spoke and the voice of God answered him.

The LORD descended to the top of Mount Sinai and called Moses to the top of the mountain. So Moses went up and the LORD said to him, "Go down and warn the people so they do not force their way through to see the LORD and many of them perish.

Even the priests, who approach the LORD, must consecrate themselves, or the LORD will break out against them."

But why all the smoke and mirrors? I think it was simply for the purpose of making an impression on the people by giving them a visual demonstration of power. God gave the Israelites many new rules to follow, and he wanted them to know that he was serious. The following excerpt indicates that Moses also thought that this was the purpose:

Exodus 20: 18-21

When the people saw the thunder and lightning and heard the trumpet and saw the mountain in smoke, they trembled with fear. They stayed at a distance and said to Moses, "Speak to us yourself and we will listen. But do not have God speak to us or we will die."
Moses said to the people, "Do not be afraid. God has come to test you, so that the fear of God will be with you to keep you from sinning."

The people remained at a distance, while Moses approached the thick darkness where God was.

Yet another example of cloud and fire being used to describe what the people saw:

Exodus 24: 15-18
When Moses went up on the mountain, the cloud covered it, and the glory of the LORD settled on Mount Sinai. For six days the cloud covered the mountain, and on the seventh day the LORD called to Moses from within the cloud. To the Israelites the glory of the LORD looked like a consuming fire on top of the mountain. Then Moses entered the cloud as he went on up the mountain. And he stayed on the mountain forty days and forty nights.

The Ten Commandments
Another interesting aspect of the whole story is the Ten Commandments being inscribed on tablets of stone. This writing was apparently something like the people had never seen before, and Moses describes them as being inscribed "by the finger of God" and the writing was the work of God:

Exodus 31:18
When the LORD finished speaking to Moses on Mount Sinai, he gave him the two tablets of the Testimony, the tablets of stone inscribed by the finger of God.
Exodus 32: 15-16 (NIV)
Moses turned and went down the mountain with the two tablets of the Testimony in his hands. They were inscribed on sides, front and back. The tablets were the work of God; the writing was the writing of God, engraved on the tablets.

Now I'm sure the content was from God and the engraving was done by the direction of God, but does God really have a finger that he writes with? If you look at this incident from a modern perspective, I think its well within the realm of possibilities that the same type of laser engraving that we see used to make very nice stone monuments could have been used to engrave the tablets.

Of course, we no longer have the actual tablets available, so there's no way to know for sure, but looking at it from this perspective can often make the incident seem more real and believable to us. If we understand a little bit about how things might have been done, it's easier for us to see the whole event as being something that actually happened instead of just a myth or a fictional story.

What Else Did This Craft Do?

I'd venture to guess that this craft ended up doing a lot more than the book of Exodus records. In fact, from the following passages, it seems that eventually the Israelites actually got kind of used to the strange aerial craft being around. After a while it was probably as common to them as airplanes are to anyone who lives near an airport:

Exodus 40: 33-38

Then Moses set up the courtyard around the tabernacle and altar and put up the curtain at the entrance to the courtyard. And so Moses finished the work.
Then the cloud covered the Tent of Meeting, and the glory of the LORD filled the tabernacle. Moses could not enter the Tent of Meeting because the cloud had settled upon it, and the glory of the LORD filled the tabernacle.

In all the travels of the Israelites, whenever the cloud lifted from above the tabernacle, they would set out; but if the cloud did not lift, they did not set out--until the day it lifted.

So the cloud of the LORD was over the tabernacle by day, and fire was in the cloud by night, in the sight of all the house of Israel during all their travels.

CHAPTER EIGHT
DIRECT INTERVENTION

For our next discussion let us again turn to the Christian Bible. Most religious people and Bible scholars would agree that the center point of the Christian Bible is the life and message of Jesus Christ.

Many people often wonder who he really was. Was he just another prophet? Just a man who happened to be a really good person? Or was he the very Son of God? Personally, when I read his message I see wisdom that was being put forward much before its time. He not only taught the basic spiritual principle of loving your fellow man - he also seemed to have some real insight into scientific principles:

- He demonstrated an understanding of how the human body works as evidenced by the number of healings he performed.

- He shared knowledge of future events such as the destruction of Jerusalem and catastrophic visions of the "end times" which showed precognition.

- He understood and saw spiritual forces that were at work in the world - forces that to this day many people don't even realize exist and mainstream science in our society is just beginning to study

The authors of the gospels recorded the events they saw surrounding the life of Christ in the best way they knew how. But they couldn't understand everything that they were seeing. Could looking at certain events during the life of Christ using our advanced knowledge of technology shed some light on what the authors of the Biblical gospels were witnessing?

The Star Of Bethlehem

You know what a star looks like, right? You also know what airplane lights look like, right? I'm assuming all of you could easily answer yes to both questions. Now think about this: What if you knew what stars looked like but didn't know what an airplane was? What would you call the airplane's lights? You might call them stars.

Figure 61: Star of Bethlehem

Ok, I'm going to play the part of the person who doesn't know what an airplane is. Now, if I were to tell you that last night I saw a set of flashing stars that moved across the sky, what would you say? Would you agree that they were stars, or would you tell me that I really saw an airplane?

With this in mind, look at the following passages from the Christian Bible. Remember, the wise men knew what stars were, but probably didn't know what UFOs were:

Matthew 2: 9-11

After they had heard the king, they went on their way, and the star they had seen in the east went ahead of them until it stopped over the place where the child was. When they saw the star, they were overjoyed. On coming to the house, they saw the child with his mother Mary, and they bowed down and worshiped him. Then they opened their treasures and presented him with gifts of gold and of incense and of myrrh.

We all know that stars don't move across the sky and hover over a particular house? Of course, I could be wrong about that, I hope there's an astronomer out there who will let me know the truth. So what was it that the wise men saw hovering over that house? Perhaps it was a satellite launched to keep an eye on things or maybe it was a small plane. Of course since it hovered over the stable, perhaps it could have been a helicopter with a spotlight mounted on its belly. Could it be the first UFO recorded in association with the life of Christ?

Shepherds And Angels

Before the wise men followed the Star of Bethlehem, we have this account of a strange encounter between shepherds and supernatural beings (angels):

Luke 2: 8-15

Figure 62: Shepherds were led to the manger by the angels.

And there were shepherds living out in the fields nearby, keeping watch over their flocks at night. An angel of the Lord appeared to them, and the glory of the Lord shone around them, and they were terrified. But the angel said to them, "Do not be afraid. I bring you good news of great joy that will be for all the people. Today in the town of David a Savior has been born to you; he is Christ the Lord. This will be a sign to you: You will find a baby wrapped in swaddling clothes and lying in a manger." Suddenly a great company of the heavenly host appeared with the angel, praising God and saying, "Glory to God in the highest, and on earth peace to men on whom his favor rests." When the angels had left them and gone into heaven, the shepherds said to one another, "Let's go to Bethlehem and see this thing that has happened, which the Lord has told us about."

Wow, it must have been quite a sight. Were these angels accompanied by UFOs? Maybe that's what is meant when it says they went "into heaven." And it could account for the amazing amount of light that they reported. Of course Simcha Jackobovic, the naked archeologist has researched the idea of Christ being born in a stable and finds that in fact, he was probably born in the home of a relative in the section normally reserved for animals which would have given Mary privacy which would have been sorely lacking in the main house.

Other Events During The Life Of Christ That Border on the Paranormal

These strange encounters from the sky didn't stop after the birth of Christ. In fact, they seemed to follow him throughout his time here on earth. For example, there is the question of where the voice in the following example came from:

John 12:28-30
(Jesus speaking) "...Father, glorify your name!"
Then a voice came from heaven, "I have glorified it, and will glorify it again." The crowd that was there and heard it said it had thundered; others said an angel had spoken to him.

Jesus said, "This voice was for your benefit, not mine.

The entire episode seems rather strange to say the least. The account doesn't give a weather report, but I would tend to believe that there was a low cloud cover that day. I've seen fog cover in the city where you can only see four or five stories of a building before the fog completely obscures it, even if you are standing right next to the building. Do you think maybe a craft could have been hiding in some low clouds or fog, watching Jesus speak, when it got a message to relay to the crowds? I don't take anything away from the power of God, but maybe this was one of those cases where he used extraterrestrial workers to help do his work.

Jesus' Baptism

The baptism of Jesus is also surrounded by some interesting events:

Mark 1: 9-11

At that time Jesus came from Nazareth in Galilee and was baptized by John in the Jordan. As Jesus was coming up out of the water, he saw heaven being torn open and the Spirit descending on him like a dove. And a voice came from heaven: "You are my Son, whom I love; with you I am well pleased."

Here we see another case of a voice from heaven. In this case, the gospel writer also includes a visual picture of "heaven being torn open." When I hear this phrase I envision a bright light, or some other event in the sky that the gospel writer had trouble explaining. Whatever it was, it's clear that there was something extraordinary happening in the skies that day over the Jordan River.

The Transfiguration

The event known as the "transfiguration" also contains some interesting details that the gospel writers seem to have had a difficult time putting into words:

Matthew 17: 1-8 (NIV)

After six days Jesus took with him Peter, James and John the brother of James, and led them up a high mountain by themselves. There he was transfigured before them. His face shone like the sun, and his clothes became as white as the light. Just then there appeared before them Moses and Elijah, talking with Jesus.
Peter said to Jesus, "Lord, it is good for us to be here. If you wish, I will put up three shelters--one for you, one for Moses and one for Elijah."

While he was still speaking, a bright cloud enveloped them, and a voice from the cloud said, "This is my Son, whom I love; with him I am well pleased. Listen to him!" When the disciples heard this, they fell facedown to the ground, terrified. But Jesus came and touched them. "Get up," he said. "Don't be afraid."

When they looked up, they saw no one except Jesus.

Notice how the event was enough to really scare the usually brave Peter, but Jesus remained calm. Was this something Jesus had seen before? He seemed very at ease with the whole situation. If the bright light came from some kind of craft that had landed, it may indicate that Jesus was very familiar with these craft and they were nothing new to him. Maybe this was something that actually happened often in those times where Jesus went off by himself to pray.

Jesus' Final UFO Encounter
Take a look at this next passage

Acts 1: 9-11
After he said this, he was taken up before their very eyes, and a cloud hid him from their sight. They were looking intently up into the sky as he was going, when suddenly two men dressed in white stood beside them.
"Men of Galilee," they said, "why do you stand here looking into the sky? This same Jesus, who has been taken from you into heaven, will come back in the same way you have seen him go into heaven.

The account states that a "cloud" hid him from their site. Was Jesus final departure into a UFO? From what I read here, I don't have a better explanation. If it was a UFO, was the ascension of Jesus his final UFO encounter?

Actually it was not. The men dressed in white who are recorded above tell the witnesses that Jesus will come back in the same way he left. Jesus agreed. Here's what he had to say about his return:

Matthew 26: 63-64
But Jesus remained silent. The high priest said to him, "I charge you under oath by the living God: Tell us if you are the Christ, the Son of God."
"Yes, it is as you say," Jesus replied. "But I say to all of you: In the future you will see the Son of Man sitting at the right hand of the Mighty One and coming on the clouds of heaven."

Even before he appeared before the high priest, Jesus had told his disciples the very same thing:

Matthew 24:30
"At that time the sign of the Son of Man will appear in the sky and all the nations of the earth will mourn. They will see the Son of Man coming on the clouds of the sky, with power and great glory."

Jesus "Away Team"
If the examples shown above were UFO accounts, why were these UFOs following Jesus around? Why were they so involved in his life? They obviously knew who he was and where he was from. For some insight into what the answer to this question might be, let's look at what Jesus had to say about himself:

John 18: 35-36
"Am I a Jew?" Pilate replied. "It was your people and your chief priests who handed you over to me. What is it you have done?"
Jesus said, "My kingdom is not of this world. If it were, my servants would fight to prevent my arrest by the Jews. But now my kingdom is from another place."

I wonder what other place he was referring to. If it's not of this world, what world is it from? I know, you're probably saying "Well you dummy, he's from heaven." Yes, I know that, but what does that term really mean? Jesus specifically says that he has a kingdom, and it is in a specific place.

Personally, while researching this article, that's not the most amazing thing I found. I knew that Jesus had said that about himself. Even more surprising is that wherever Jesus was from, it seems his disciples were also from. Check out the following passage where Jesus is referring specifically to the twelve apostles:

John 17:16
Here Jesus refers to his disciples saying "They are not of the world, even as I am not of it."

A very short but direct comment. Many write this off by saying that he was speaking figuratively or something like that, but I think it more likely that Jesus meant exactly what he said.

If your mind is open to the possibility that Jesus was from a kingdom that was in a specific place outside of planet earth, and that he incarnated here on a particular mission, doesn't it make sense that he'd bring along some personal assistants? This might explain some of Jesus' other actions in relation to the twelve apostles. He actually handpicked them out of a much larger group of disciples:

Luke 6:12-13
One of those days Jesus went out to a mountainside to pray, and spent the night praying to God. When morning came, he called his disciples to him and chose twelve of them, whom he also designated apostles.

Do you think that perhaps he recognized them as special workers from "his kingdom" even though they did not yet realize that fact? It's also interesting that immediately after he met some of the people who he would later bring out of a larger group to be part of the twelve apostles, Jesus called them by names other than their earth-given names. The man whose parents had named "Simon son of John" Jesus instead chose to call "Cephas" which can be translated into the name we still call him today - "Peter" (see John 1:42).

He called James and John the "Sons of Thunder" (Mark 3:17) - maybe that was a nickname they got in his kingdom and Jesus was referring to it then to help them recall that. This kind of "mission recall," even at a subconscious level in the minds of the disciples, could also help explain why the twelve apostles are described as immediately dropping their entire careers and following this then relatively unknown person who was roaming around the countryside.

Angelic Armies
Jesus seemed to be talking about a real kingdom as he also made it clear that wherever his kingdom was, there were plenty of troops standing by and available at a moment's notice if he decided to call on them:

Matthew 26:53

"Do you think I cannot call on my Father, and he will at once put at my disposal more than twelve legions of angels?"

In fact, these angelic forces are recorded as assisting him a number of times during his mission on earth. They were there to assist him after his temptation in the desert:

Matthew 4:10-11

Jesus said to him, "Away from me, Satan! For it is written: 'Worship the Lord your God, and serve him only.' "Then the devil left him, and angels came and attended him.

Mark 1:13

...and he was in the desert forty days, being tempted by Satan. He was with the wild animals, and angels attended him.

They were there in the Garden of Gethsemane when Jesus was wrestling with completing the final stages of his earthly mission:

Luke 22:42-44

"Father, if you are willing, take this cup from me; yet not my will, but yours be done." An angel from heaven appeared to him and strengthened him. And being in anguish, he prayed more earnestly, and his sweat was like drops of blood falling to the ground.

Finally, the angels assisted with the task of helping his disciples realize that he had indeed risen from the dead as he had promised:

Matthew 28: 2-4

There was a violent earthquake, for an angel of the Lord came down from heaven and, going to the tomb, rolled back the stone and sat on it. His appearance was like lightning, and his clothes were white as snow. The guards were so afraid of him that they shook and became like dead men.

Luke 24:4-8
While they were wondering about this, suddenly two men in clothes that gleamed like lightning stood beside them. In their fright the women bowed down with their faces to the ground, but the men said to them, "Why do you look for the living among the dead? He is not here; he has risen! Remember how he told you, while he was still with you in Galilee: 'The Son of Man must be delivered into the hands of sinful men, be crucified and on the third day be raised again.'"

Then they remembered his words.

"Then they remembered his words" - interesting to note here that even though Jesus clearly taught his disciples what was going to happen, his disciples didn't quite understand it until they saw it actually happen. A similar thing has happened throughout history with the whole UFO phenomenon being associated with Jesus hasn't it? For ages people have read the same Bible that you and I have today but never associated UFOs with any of the events. How could they have until UFO events started to become part of the common person's reality? Today just about everyone has at least heard of UFOs whether they believe they are real or not. We are finally starting to get the information that we need to begin making the connection.

Did Jesus Refer To Non Angelic Off-Planet Followers
Here is another interesting statement that was made by Jesus in John 10:16. Jesus said "I have other sheep that are not of this sheep pen. I must bring them also. They too will listen to my voice, and there shall be one flock and one shepherd."

This was certainly a very interesting statement. Of course, this passage can be interpreted to mean that he was concerned about people outside of Israel, if Israel was what he was referring to when he said "this sheep pen." But what if the sheep pen that he was referring to was the planet earth? If this is what he meant, he may well have been referring to a desire for a day when his followers who resided off-planet would be united with those on earth who will choose to follow his teachings.

Another Interpretation
We've heard Jesus' testimony about who he was, and that he claimed to be of a kingdom not on this earth, that he came from above. But Jesus also realized that self-promotion could only go so far. As he put it:

John 5:31-34
"If I testify about myself, my testimony is not valid. There is another who testifies in my favor, and I know that his testimony about me is valid. You have sent to John and he has testified to the truth. Not that I accept human testimony; but I mention it that you may be saved."

He was referring here to the testimony of John the Baptist. Let's take a look at what he says about Jesus to see if he might hint at an extraterrestrial origin:

John 3:31-32
"The one who comes from above is above all; the one who is from the earth belongs to the earth, and speaks as one from the earth. The one who comes from heaven is above all. He testifies to what he has seen and heard, but no one accepts his testimony."

John the Baptist seems to make it clear that Jesus does not belong to the earth, and actually calls him "the one who comes from heaven." Interesting how he notes that Jesus testifies to what he has seen and heard. Where would

Jesus have seen and heard these things? John makes it clear that his message was not from planet earth, but he was bringing a message to planet earth from somewhere else.

I'd imagine that much of Jesus' testimony that John is referring to might not have been recorded in the scriptures, or might have been edited out at a later time. Maybe he gave his actual disciples even clearer accounts of his origins that they knew people of the time wouldn't understand but they put enough hints in their accounts that once we were aware of the modern UFO phenomenon we could begin to figure it out. As far as the topic of UFOs in the Bible, even though we have a number of accounts that could be UFOs in our current Bible, we can be sure that there were many more in the actual life of Christ. Take the following example where Jesus is talking to the disciple Nathanael:

John 1:50-52
Jesus said, "You believe because I told you I saw you under the fig tree. You shall see greater things than that." He then added, "I tell you the truth, you shall see heaven open, and the angels of God ascending and descending on the Son of Man."

Nowhere in the Gospels is this event actually recorded, but if we take Jesus at his word, it must have happened sometime during Nathanael's lifetime. Kind of makes you wonder how many other extraordinary events like this never made it into our current version of the Bible.

What Does All This Mean?
Now if UFOs were involved in the life of Jesus, the implications are astounding. Maybe that's why most churches don't want to deal with the whole issue. But every day the evidence of alien visitors to our planet becomes stronger and stronger. Could some of these visitors be

working for the same Jesus Christ that we know from the Biblical record?

CHAPTER NINE
NON-HUMANS AMONG US

So the first part of this book has dealt with the involvement of what we call unidentified flying objects with the religions of earth. Every miracle that has been described by the prophets and those who wrote the scriptures could easily have been the result of advanced scientific methods. It also covered interaction between flying things and miraculous acts of the gods. Now we are going to look at the possibility that other races, perhaps described by our religious leaders as demons live, or have lived on this planet.

If as is proposed, there are descendants of an alien race that lives among us and actually manipulates both people as well as governments, then there must over the eons been some signs of them. Well in fact there have been, we just have been too busy to notice them.

John A. Keel, in his book 'Our Haunted Planet,[33]', gives an interesting introduction to the reality of an alien race that allegedly has taken careful measures to remain hidden from the mass consciousness of those dwelling on the surface of planet earth -- or those ignorant 'human cattle' whom they are intent on manipulating and exploiting from their secret hiding places above, below and even amongst the inhabitants of planet earth:

"...The parahuman Serpent People of the past are still among us. They were probably worshipped by the builders of Stonehenge and the forgotten ridge-making cultures of South America. "...

In some parts of the world the Serpent People successfully posed as gods and imitated the techniques of the super-intelligence. This led to the formation of pagan religions centered on placating these gods, and very often resulted this placation took the form of human sacrifices. The conflict, so far as man himself was concerned, became one of religions and races. Whole civilizations based upon the worship of these false gods rose and fell in Asia, Africa,

---

[33] Keel, John, Our Haunted Planet, Galde Press, Inc.; Revised edition (May 1, 1999)

and South America. The battleground had been chosen, and the mode of conflict had been decided upon.

The human race would supply the pawns to be used, and abused, in these wars of the gods. The mode of control exercised by the gods was complicated as usual. Human beings were largely free of direct control due to free will. Therefore, each individual had to consciously commit himself, or herself, to one of the opposing forces. As a result, the main battle became one for control of what we call the human soul.

Figure 63: Serpent People

Once an individual had committed himself, or herself, to a particular belief, he opened a door of some sort so that an indefinable something could actually enter his body and exercise some control over his subconscious mind.

Figure 64: The Hindu's talked of the Serpent People

Many researchers believe that what became known as the Serpent People or OMEGA Group, attacked man in various ways, trying to rid the planet of him. But the super-intelligence was still able to look over man. God worked out new ways of communication and control, always in conflict with the Serpent People. There are a number of researchers who have claimed that the story of the serpent in the Garden of Eden actually referred to one of the Serpent People.

There have also been a number of stories told in relation to these 'Serpent People', maintaining that some of these creatures are now living among us and have been doing so for a very long time. There is an individual who is believed to be an anonymous Intelligence officer who is referred to as 'Commander X'. He has recently released details of an incident which may well have come right out of a John Carpenter movie, if not for the fact that the Commander himself, from his own high-security position within the Intelligence Community, is convinced of its potential reality:

Another story comes from a service member, a private, stationed on the surface at Dulce, New Mexico. Though most privates tend to mind their own business, this young man soon realized something mighty 'odd' was going on around there, but it took a while for him to put his finger on it. According to a statement that the private later gave to several researchers who put him in touch with Commander X:

Figure 65: View down a tunnel at Dulce, New Mexico

"'One morning last September, I was working on a routine job when another of the young enlistees, a mechanic, came in with a small rush job he wanted welded at once. He had the print and proceeded to show me exactly what he wanted. We are both bending over the bench in front of the welder when I happened to look directly into his face. It seemed to suddenly become covered with a semi-transparent film or cloud. His features faded and in their place appeared a 'thing' with bulging eyes, no hair and scales for skin. I stood and looked at it for about 20 seconds. Whatever it was stood and looked at me without moving. Then the strange face seemed to fade away, and at the same time recede into the ordinary face of the young man underneath. The dissipation of the imposed face lasted or took about five seconds before it was completely gone and I was standing there weak, my mouth open and staring at the young man who had come in with the rush order. The young 'man' did not seem to be conscious of the elapsed *time when I had observed all this but went right on talking about the job as if nothing had happened."*

"*'This is hard to take but I assure you it was still harder for me. No one can realize a jolt you could get from seeing anything like this until they have experienced it for themselves. It was several days before I had myself convinced that maybe after all what I had seen was real and that I was not suffering from illusions and the beginning of insanity. Days passed before I saw this particular phenomenon again. The next time was later at night at the guard house near the front gate, on the way to work. I had purchased some small items and on arriving I went around to the guard house with my slip to retrieve my package. There was only one guard on duty. I handed him the check and he began to look at the package, taking his time. I waited a minute, then happened to look directly at him again. His face began to change. Again a face of a strange creature was imposed. You could see through the imposed face for a few seconds and then it became the only one visible [solidified is the word] and again about 20 seconds duration. Again five seconds for dissipation and the guard started to move normally again, found my package and gravely handed it to me and I walked out without a word being said.'*"

Since coming across this report from the 'Commander', a number of researchers have made an effort to see if there were any other similar accounts that might confirm the existence of 'Chameleons' or alien 'infiltrators' working on the surface of planet earth in an apparent attempt to pass themselves off as human beings and blend-in with our society, for whatever nefarious agenda they might be serving. Some of the reports of quasi-human infiltrators spoke of the "Men In Black" who have terrorized UFO witnesses. Although many of the 'M.I.B.' who have been reported were obviously humans working for some obscure governmental surface, other-planetary or subterranean intelligence agency as well as others that appeared to be either cyborgs, clones or even paraphysical manifestations, there was a branch of the so-called MIB which betrayed definite reptilian characteristics.

These in essence were reptilian humanoids with a full-blown -- although at times not-too-convincing -- 'reconstructive surgery' job, apparently intended to allow them to operate in human society undetected. Some of the early 'infiltrators' betrayed themselves with their 'plastic' or artificial appearance, whereas in more recent years the 'disguise' has become far more sophisticated with the advent of molecular shape-shifting occult-technology, techno-hypnotic transmitters, and portable laser-hologram technology, and as a result, they are harder to detect. However there are ways.

George Andrews, in his book *Extraterrestrial Friends and Foes*,[34] quotes a statement made by Valdamar Valerian, director of Leading Edge Research:

"*A friend of mine and four of his friends experimented with crystalline structures a year or two ago (mid-1980's - Branton), and they figured out how to cut them along certain planes so they could actually see the aura or energy field around people. That's when they*

---

[34] Andrews, George, <u>Extraterrestrial Friends and Foes</u>, ILLUMINET PRESS., P.O. Box 2808., Lilburn, GA 30226.

discovered that all people aren't 'people', or the people they thought they were. It appears that some E.T. humanoids have a dark blue ovoid aura. (Note: Aura cameras developed by Chuck Shramek -- the same Chuck Shramek of the 'Hale-Bopp Companion' controversy -- and others clearly show the 7 multi-colored 'chakra' points of the human soul/spirit matrix. Presumably since reptilians have NO soul, they would have NO multicolored auric field.) It so happens that all the people they checked that met this criterion also wore dark glasses and made every attempt to act like they really wanted nothing to do with people in general.

"They followed one of these people out into the desert where he evidently had a trailer. After waiting until dusk, they made a pretense of needing help and knocked on the door. After a short while, the light went on and the man came to the door. He looked normal, except that his pupils were vertical slits instead of circles. It works. The only trouble is that it costs $2,000 to put a pair of those glasses together..."

There have been a lot of stories that several areas across the Western U.S. where surface and/or underground military installations exist have reportedly produced similar 'Chameleon' sightings. There seems to be a trend which involves the infiltration of the NSA-CIA and the subsequent 'replacement' of agency personnel, and in turn military-Industrial personnel, by alien life forms not loyal to planet earth nor to the human race in general. These reports are very similar to other reports that made the rounds within 'fringe' research groups during the early

1980's concerning the reported 'assimilation' of high-ranking Communist officials and scientists by serpent-like humanoids, reptilian beings that were reputedly revived out of suspended animation from a frozen city that was discovered under the northern Siberian ice fields. This incident was referred to as the "Siberian Affair".

Aside from Dulce, New Mexico and the Nevada Test Site, other areas where these "chameleon" sightings are said to have taken place include Deep Springs, CA and Dugway, Utah. Dugway Proving Ground (DPG) is a US Army facility located approximately 85 miles southwest of Salt Lake City, Utah in southern Tooele County and just north of Juab County. A woman by the name of Barbara, who worked as a hair stylist at a salon near the proving grounds claimed she saw one of the high ranking military officials transform temporarily into an entity with 'reptilian' features.

Another source at Dugway who worked in an auto shop claimed that he saw a similar phenomenon while changing the tires on the car of one Dugway military official. Remember that Dugway works closely with

Figure 66: Moth man

Area 51, which is just to the west and across the state border in Nevada. It is interesting that there are claims that the joint CIA-alien activity within the 'Dreamland' underground complexes of Nevada have and are being extended to the underground facilities below the St. George and Dugway areas of Utah, among other sites.

Another 'sighting' of these shape shifters is said to have occurred just south of the mid-point of an old toll road that ran between Hopland and Lakeport, California. The sighting involved large black automobiles[35] that would leave and enter a dead-end road in the area. When investigated, the tire tracks ran right up and under a large boulder at the base of a cliff and seemingly disappeared beneath it, and since the road was fenced on one side and a steep hill existed on the other, it is unlikely that the large automobiles were able to turn around.

This same area, especially one particular mountain there, is known as a very unusual place. 'Bottomless' caves with stone stairwells have been reported by explorers. Government vehicles and personnel have 'disappeared' without a trace on the road. An 'atmosphere of fear' is said to exist in an area approximately 30 miles in diameter. Also there have been a lot of unexplained deaths among the settlers in the area. Apparently this area is the site of a large underground center of 'alien' activity. This activity was taking place back in the 1930's, long before the so-called alien "Men In Black" started getting any major attention from Ufologists in America.

The Dulce enigma [and the "chameleons"] have not only infiltrated Utah, Nevada and California, but seems to have stretched its tentacles all the way up to the Pacific Northwest. One area of particular interest is the Madigan Military Hospital south of Seattle, Washington near FORT LEWIS... which has been investigated by Val Valerian. In June of 1992 Valerian released the following article, titled

---

[35] Many reported Men In Black sightings are said to involve 1949 black Cadillac's.

"*ALIEN INFILTRATION OF THE MILITARY MEDICAL SYSTEM: MADIGAN HOSPITAL IN WASHINGTON*", in his LEADING EDGE newsletter. According to the report:

"About a year ago, we ran into several people who stated that they 'had heard' that 'reptilian humanoids were working at a U.S. Army Hospital near Fort Lewis, Washington. At that point, these statements were simply filed away in 'rumor' status, pending the arrival of something more substantial. Descriptions of the nature of and appearance of alien humanoid forms that could be termed 'reptilian' vary widely. Reptilian humanoids have been described in Italy as looking very lizard like, even some with tails. Pictures showing some of these entities were published in an Italian magazine and eventually ended up in the United States in 'The Leading Edge'.

"Logic would seem to tell us that if alien humanoids were in fact in 'collusion' with military medical personnel at a hospital, they would not in fact have the appearance of anything other than humans, or be close enough to humans to blend in. About a month ago, the nature of synchronicity brought me to an espresso bar, where I chanced to engage a lady in her early 50's in some small conversation about an entirely unrelated matter. She had been a nurse for some twenty years, and sixteen of those twenty years had been spent working for the U.S. Army. She retired from the service and was now job hunting in the local area. She was very professional, and seemed to know a lot about the nursing field.

Gradually, her (for ease of understanding let's call her Betty)

Bldg 9040
Fitzsimmons Drive
Tacoma, WA 98431

Directory
Assistance
(253) 968-1110 DSN 782

Figure 67: Madigan Military Medical Center

conversation got around to a 'very unusual place', Madigan Military Hospital, which is located on Route 5 south of Seattle. She had applied for work at the hospital and noticed that it was indeed a hospital unlike any she had ever seen before. Madigan is a brand new $150 million dollar facility, built about a year or so ago. From her description, there are small R2D2-type robots that shuttle prescriptions between floors; all the equipment is prototype 'one-of-a-kind', like laser x-rays and a lot of equipment that was extremely high tech. It was not this alone which peaked my interest, but a comment she made later. She made the statement that when she entered a specific lab in the hospital she noticed that all the personnel were extremely absorbed in their work -- nothing too uncommon about that. But then she stated that she had the thought that some of the equipment looked quite 'alien', and two men who looked exactly alike turned and looked at her in response to her thought. She said that the eyes of these two men were quite penetrating and that they both seemed to move in unison. That got Val's interest. She then stated that during the tour of the facility, the individual who was escorting her said that the top floor of the hospital and two of the sub-basement floors were Top Secret Research and Development areas and were off limits to both military and civilian personnel. That really got Val's attention.

"Subsequently," continued the article, "Val ran into a cable repairman who was installing cable TV in a nearby town, and decided on a hunch to mention to him about the strange nature of Madigan. The hunch paid off. He said he had been involved in the installation of fiber optic networks between the floors of the hospital when it was in its construction stage, and that there was a three foot space in between the floors where the optics ran.

"Since these observations were the result of her [the nurse Betty's] preliminary interview, Val talked to her about the idea of getting more information, since she would be going back at least one more time. She agreed to make some tapes of her observations. The transcript of these tapes is as follows:

VISIT TO MADIGAN HOSPITAL

The entrance to Madigan hospital is off of Interstate 5 past Olympia, Washington. The exit is marked as 'Madigan Hospital, Camp Murray Exit'. As you enter the area the hospital sits to the right -- a massive white structure. As you enter the parking lot, there is a pond and sunken area that runs through a bridge which connects the 'medical mall' area to a three story building that serves as the main core of the hospital, where the services like x-ray, nuclear medicine and other services are performed.

The three story complex is connected to an eight-story tower dubbed 'the nursing tower. The tower has a floor that is closed off, and Betty was never able to find access to it. (What follows are Betty's words)"

"'I entered the front of the hospital, and the lobby was very typical, but not typical of a hospital of this size. I then went to the information desk and was greeted by an 'oriental' Specialist 4th Class, who was seated. He seemed very low key and laid back. I was directed to Human Resources.

"'As I walked through the corridors, I noticed how beautiful and calm I was beginning to feel. The colors are very soft and conducive to feeling mellow.

"'The military personnel were very slow moving [which has NOT been my experience in the past, having served five years as an Army nurse], and low key. I went to the Human Resources and asked about an application, and was directed to a Master Sergeant who was the director of personnel.

"'Having been a medical technologist for the better part of 25 years, the equipment I saw at the hospital was far beyond anything I have ever seen. I was shown an area where there was a long room with computer banks on both sides where both civilian and military personnel were working. Before entering the room, I was asked to stand in front of the door, where I was scanned by some beam-like light. I was told that my thermal pattern was being recorded in order to permit my entry to the room.

"'Off this room was another room where procedures were conducted on patients, and I noticed that a patient walked over and climbed on an exam table. The procedure they were doing always requires that the patient must be sedated, however I noticed that they physician leaned over the patient and touched the patient in the center of the forehead with his index and middle finger of one hand. Immediately, the patient fell into a state off sedation and the procedure was started. What kind of doctor can touch a patient in that way and sedate him?

"'I looked around at the other personnel in the room at this time. There were two, a Private First Class and a Specialist 4th Class at opposite ends of the room from where I was standing. Both of these men were the same size, had the same skin color and moved in a very deliberate manner. I was talking with the Sergeant and happened to say something to myself very softly while having the thought how strange these people seemed. Both of the men turned and looked at me almost as if to stare at me. I got this very strange feeling.

I had heard before from a friend whose brother had made the uncharacteristic comment that 'aliens worked at Madigan. All the people in the room and the military personnel in general that I had seen in the hospital seemed to move very, very slowly, almost in slow motion. I left the area and went back to the Sergeant's office.

"'A month later, I returned to Madigan with a friend to see, without telling her anything of my experience, if she saw and felt the same things I did. She is very sensitive to variations in electromagnetic fields, and eventually had a headache and became nauseated. There are many other *things about this place. Between the floors there are spaces where small robots move to deliver supplies to all the wards and other areas in the hospital, according to the Sergeant. I was told that there is no reason for personnel to go into these areas -- that the robots do all that. I did see one of the robot devices. It looked like the R2D2 character on 'star wars'.*

"'My friend and I entered through what is known as the clinic mall. This area houses the outpatient clinic. There were very few people there for such a large clinic. We were told that there are three floors beneath the hospital and one floor above that are off limits to all personnel, military and civilian, and that these areas were classified Top Secret and were research and development [R&D] areas. There are very unusual antennas on top of the hospital. The three-story main service area has a complex on top of it that appears to have no entrance and no windows. Judging from the way the hospital is built, there are a lot of 'dead areas' that comprise spaces that cannot be accessed from the main service area.

"'The personal feeling we both got being in the hospital was that we started to feel very drained, and we both experienced getting a dull headache. It wasn't until we had driven several miles from the facility that we started to feel better.'"

In the research for this book, this author came across yet another report suggesting that reptilian entities were infiltrating our military-industrial complex, however the exact source of this particular story was not confirmed and therefore should be taken as is. The report stated that sometime during the 1980's a young lady working as a secretary in the Pentagon noticed a high-ranking Pentagon 'official' who had apparently lost a contact lens. A quick glimpse showed her that the eye from where the lens fell out was not human, but instead contained a vertically-slit pupil. No one working at the Pentagon seemed to know where the high ranking official that had lost the contact lens worked although everyone he came in contact with had apparently assumed that he was supposed to be there in some capacity or another.

The Secretary however informed her superiors of the strange incident, and immediately Security Personnel approached the 'officer' who apparently was not aware of his missing contact lens. The 'man' did not make any major attempts to resist. According to reports the secretary heard later, when the apartment of this 'official' was searched, copies of several sensitive documents on the "Star Wars" or "Strategic Defense Initiative" program were discovered. Apparently the entity had been stealing the documents and transmitting their contents to some point beyond the planet. Rumor had it that the entity was physically examined and it was discovered that its internal organs were not human.

In reference to the Draconian interest in our planetary defense net, let's look at the following information from British Ufologists Timothy Good[36], who described the unfortunate fate of several experts who assisted in the development of the Star Wars (SDI) defense system. Apparently, they were either eliminated by those they worked for so that they would not reveal what they knew, or someone or something 'else' that was not pleased

---

[36] Good, Timothy, Need to Know: UFOs, the Military, and Intelligence, Pegasus Books (November 15, 2007).

with the ultimate products of their efforts was responsible for their tragic deaths. Certainly, all of these scientists dying at once cannot be explained in coincidental terms, whatever the case:

"Reports of suspicious deaths, darkly and deeply linked to UFO's, persist, however, and continue to cause speculation. Word comes from Gordon Creighton, editor of the informative Flying Saucer Review, who notes a possible deathly tie-in with the U.S. 'Star Wars' program. He wrote to Timothy Good in Nov. 1988 as follows:

"*'here in Britain 22 scientists have reportedly either taken their own lives or died in very strange or mysterious circumstances. And it seems that most... were engaged in British work on behalf of, or related to the U.S. 'Star Wars' program. The British government, it seems, was trying to hush it up. But press statements here say that the U.S. government had put our government on the spot and demanded a full inquiry. So, quite clearly, it is either the Russians or THEM...'*

"As many researchers have surmised, 'Star Wars', ostensibly conceived as a defensive system against Russian missile attack, may have had from its beginning a 'defensive' UFO connection. Whatever the case, a 'mock test' in September, 1988, of an earth-shattering warhead -- much like 'Star Wars' in reverse -- was conducted at the Tonopah Test Range in Nevada. Announced as a proposed super-weapon designed to destroy 'Russian' underground command centers dug in solid rock down to 1,000 [feet], some UFO analysts believe that the real target is not Russian but another adversary deep down in cavernous installations in Nevada and New Mexico.

"According to the Pentagon, the proposed earth-penetrating warhead is 'urgently needed'. According to rumor-mills, an alien race -- the 'grays' -- in their fortified underground laboratories, are genetically experimenting with the human race. Even more ominous, rumors say that their intransigence today may lead to new perils tomorrow."

MORE ODD STORIES

In reference to the "Chameleons" and certain elements of the so-called "Men In Black" phenomena, the following account from Brazil puts everything in perspective. The following excerpts were taken from a report by Brazilian researcher Antonio Huneeus, titled: "THE 'CHUPAS' -- UFO HORROR STORIES FROM BRAZIL". Mr. Huneeus describes the following incident that was investigated by APEX[37] in Sao Paulo, one of the best known UFO groups in Brazil, founded by Dr. Max Berezowsky:

"...The affair began near Vitoria, the capitol of [the] state of Espiritu Santo north of Rio state, where there are beaches rich in mineral contents. It happened either in late 1979 or early 1980, [Osni] Schwarz wasn't sure, when he told the story in 1986...

"A youngster called Aeromar sold beverages at the beach, where one day he encountered three men dressed with suits and ties -- highly unusual clothing for the beach, especially in Brazil -- who approached him and said they wanted to talk to him. Aeromar became scared, thinking they were perhaps policemen who wanted to implicate him

---

[37] Association of Extraterrestrial Investigations

in a drug case, so he avoided the beach for a few days. As he returned home after dropping off his girlfriend one night, he saw a car with the same three men inside. He ran to the house, but suddenly he couldn't hear well. His mother took him to the hospital where he was not cured, although about a month later he suddenly could hear well again.

"Aeromar moved to Rio, finding work at a bakery in a shift between 4 and 11 PM. One night, as he was crossing one of the many TUNNELS that link the Rio bays, he saw two of the MIB's walking in his direction. The youngster ran in the opposite direction, only to find the third MIB waiting at a bus stop. He escaped and went back to the bakery, where he told his boss that the Vitoria police were chasing him. The boss accompanied him to the nearest police station to make a complaint, which he did, but he was not believed. The boss then convinced him that he should perhaps move to Sao Paulo, a bigger city where it may be easier to go unnoticed.

"So Aeromar moved to Sao Paulo, finding work in an electrical company and sharing a room with another man. He also became friends with a vendor of beverages from Vitoria who had a stand near a movie theater. While hanging out there one night, a car stopped right in front of the stand and the door opened.

"Even though he didn't want to go, Aeromar lost his will and entered the car. The door closed and he found inside -- not surprisingly -- the three same men whom he had been dodging for months. They drove for a while, leaving the city and entering a wooded area.

"The car stopped and they all walked up to a big UFO surrounded by some sort of luminous ring and hovering above the ground. The men walked underneath the craft, which emitted a ray of light and they suddenly were inside. Still drained of any willpower, Aeromar walked to a chair and sat down. From the arms of the chair appeared handles that secured his wrists. An iron bar then pressed his forehead backwards while another gadget fastened his neck. Up to here the men were always dressed with suits, but at this point an incredible transformation took place: the MIB'S head ripped opened into a heart shape and the skin became green and scaled like a Reptilian. Take into account that while the popular image of the MIB was well known 14 years ago, the idea of reptilian abductors was then not in vogue as nowadays.

"Be that as it may, the UFOnauts proceeded to interrogate and tell him things that were going to happen both to him and the earth. To make the story even more 'Hollywoodesque', a door in the room opened at one point and Aeromar was able to peek at human corpses hanging by their feet from hooks. The man naturally became traumatized, remembering only that his straps were loosened. Everything went blank after that...

"Aeromar's conscious recollection places him next back at the theater, but several hours later since there was no traffic in the streets. He returned to his room in panic and began to tell the story to his roommate. A strange force pushed his body, however, throwing it against the wall in front of him, as he remembered the aliens had told him that he shouldn't speak about the experience or he would suffer. Aeromar cried for a while, not knowing what to do. A few *days later, his friend contacted the Globo TV network, which was working on a UFO documentary. Globo, in turn, passed the tip to Dr. Max Berezowsky. Aeromar and his roommate went to APEX on a very busy day when the office was full of people. They told the whole story to Dr. Berezowsky and a few assistants, Osni Schwarz among them.*

"Berezowsky attempted to do hypnotic regression with the witness, but there was too much interference in the office and Aeromar was in total panic. He was saying that 'they' were going to take him on the next Thursday and that a UFO was going to land in a Sao Paulo neighborhood on Tuesday night. A crowd of people, in fact, went that night to the supposed landing site but nothing happened. Although Dr. Berezowsky was in touch with Aeromar, He vanished a few days later and nobody ever saw him again.'"

So after all of this, is it possible that this is the secret that is at the core of the ultimate secret society and thus motivates all secret societies? This secret would seem to be that over us, and among us it seems, is a more advanced race of beings that earlier were treated as gods and seemingly worked miracles.

So what are these secret societies working for? Perhaps it is the complete and total control of the human race, a control that they had firmly in hand eons ago. Clearly, they have the ability to manipulate time and space as well as many things we perceive.

CHAPTER TEN
AGENTS OF THE UNSEEN

So now would be a good time for the reader to consider what to think about the scenario that has been laid out in the previous chapters. Is it really so hard to believe that this world is being manipulated by a super-secret organization that operates form the shadows, controlling the very mechanisms that make our society function. Are we the dominate species on this planet as we have always believed or are we merely the unwitting servants of an incredibly old, incredibly powerful ancient order? Are we the masters of all that we survey or the servants being watched over by what we call UFOs?

As if this is not enough for the reader to digest, there is still more that will certainly be considered bizarre. It is the belief of many that this advanced race of masters also uses what we refer to as the paranormal to influence humans.

Now this author does not think that there is anyone who would not agree that religion is a very strong control mechanism. No matter what the religion or who the "god" there is always a long list of dos and don'ts. Religions have been responsible for more wars, death and destruction than almost any other cause. Religion has been responsible for the destruction of entire civilizations and the death or millions of innocent lives. If the "gods" created religions, then it makes sense that we are all taught that we much obey the wishes of the gods. However, what about those who are not religious, how are they controlled or at least influenced. Perhaps for those individuals there are the paranormal, the world of the unseen.

We are all well aware of the familiar world around us, but few seem aware that there is an entirely different world that is generally referred to as the world of the paranormal. Now, with the dozens of books and the many television shows about ghosts and goblins, there is no doubt that most are aware of certain aspects of this other world, but there is a vast world of the unseen that is still a mystery to most.

Actually, for as long as there have been tales of hauntings and ghostly phenomena, there have been sightings of strange entities that people have come to refer to as the 'Shadow People'. These Shadow People are defined by their featureless, shadow-like appearance and the feeling of foreboding that most experience when these mysterious creatures are

Figure 68: General description of a shadow person

present. These shadows are nearly always described by witnesses as having a manly shape, large and with a broad silhouette and perhaps the strangest thing about them, is that they are usually seen wearing a hat of some sort. In some instances there are red eyes that seem to pierce right through you.

This author is the host of the Ken Hudnall Show[38] a paranormal radio show heard on http://www.borderlandradio.com. Callers to the show have related numerous stories of encounters with Shadow People. No one is ever sure exactly what the Shadow People are, but there seem little doubt that they are not 'normal ghosts'? Most people will say that they are not like anything they have ever seen. In fact, these entities don't usually seem to have purpose to their visits and from the bad feelings they emit, it seems that they aren't benign by any means.

Figure 69: Two common versions of shadow people.

One important observation about shadow people, that isn't often seen with 'conventional ghosts' is that they seem to be very much aware of our presence. A lot of the time manifestations occur involving an entity that seems to be going about daily business; rarely do they

---

[38] The Ken Hudnall Show is heard Monday through Friday from 6:00-9:00 PM Mountain Time on http://www.blogtalkradio.com/ken-hudnall.

notice or try and communicate with people. The Shadow People tend to be very aware of our presence and in fact seem like they wish to make us feel uncomfortable or frightened. They do not attempt to communication, they merely allow themselves to be seen which may in and of itself be a method of communication.

There are many experts who refuse to classify Shadow people with ghosts claiming they are a separate phenomenon for several reasons as outlined below:

- First, they claim that the movement of shadow people is said to be quick and jerky, sometimes with stops, starts, and changes of direction, not at all like the smooth floating motion often associated with ghost sighting. This is apparently the primary reason they are usually seen out of the corner of the eye.

- Second, some people report being able to discern that the shadow people are wearing a fedora style hat like a 1930's-era gangster or a cloak.

- Third, shadow people usually appear quite solid, unlike the ephemeral appearance of ghosts.

- Fourth, there are very few reports of positive interactions with shadow people.

Unlike the friendly ghost sightings that are fairly common, encounters with shadow folk are almost always frightening or shocking. In fact, even the experts that view shadow men as a subset of ghosts usually concede that shadow men are malignant beings.

The real question is whether or not these shadow creatures are evil? It is tempting to say that they are, especially given the bad vibes they seem to let off to anyone with whom they come in contact. However, there is not much documentation to say that a bad occurrence usually follows a Shadow Man visitation. If fact, most visitations usually result in the apparition fading away, or disappearing when noticed. They never seem to talk or approach the witness; instead they simply are seen standing menacingly in doorways and corners.

Some people say that Shadow People are aliens or time traveling beings. This is an interesting theory, as it suggests that not only do these entities exist, but they are frequently visitors in our lives. There is the question as to why they seem to want to hang around us so much? Are we being studied by these creatures? Could this be why there are so many reports of 'feelings of evil' coming from these creatures?

What makes the Shadow People phenomena interesting, in the world of the supernatural, is the consistency in the sightings. No matter whether it's an old person or a child, or someone at any age in between, what they see is always the same. People on opposite ends of the world report seeing these entities on a daily basis and their recollections are strikingly similar. Whatever these Shadow People are they are definitely a regular occurrence in a lot of people's lives.

The beginnings of a visitation are always the same. You were sitting comfortably on your sofa reading the latest issue of FATE in the dim light when movement across the room caught your attention. It seemed dark and shadowy, but there was nothing there. You returned to your reading - and a moment later there it was again. You looked up quickly this time and saw the fleeting but distinctly human shape of the shadow pass quickly over the far wall... and disappear.

What was that? Some natural shadow? Your heightened imagination? A ghost? Or was it something that seems to be a spreading phenomenon - apparitions that are coming to be known as "shadow people" or "shadow beings." Perhaps this is an old phenomenon with a new name that is now being discussed more openly, in part thanks to the Internet. Or maybe it's a phenomenon that, for some reason, is manifesting with greater frequency and intensity now.

Those who are experiencing and studying the shadow people phenomenon say that these entities almost always used to be seen out of the corner of the eye and very briefly. But more and more, people are beginning to see them straight on

Figure 70: Are Shadow People and Aliens connected?

and for longer periods of time. Some experiencers testify that they have even seen eyes, usually red, on these shadow beings.

The mysterious sightings have become a hot topic of conversion in paranormal chat rooms, message boards and websites, and it is given widespread attention on paranormal talk radio. However, there have been other tales of Shadow People appearing immediately after the occupants of the dwelling have had contact with UFOs. Is this coincidence or perhaps a result of the contact?

What are shadow people and where do they come from? Several theories have been offered.

THE IMAGINATION

The explanation we get from skeptics and mainstream science - and who are usually people who have never experienced the shadow people phenomenon - is that it is nothing more than the active human imagination. It's our minds playing tricks on us... our eyes seeing things in a fraction of a second that aren't really there - illusions... real shadows caused by passing auto headlights, or some similar explanation. And without a doubt, these explanations probably can account for some if not many experiences. The human eye and mind are easily fooled. But can they account for all cases?

GHOSTS

To call these entities ghosts demands first a definition of what we mean by ghosts. (See the article: Ghosts: What Are They?) But by almost any definition, shadow people are somewhat different than ghost phenomena. Whereas ghost apparitions are almost always a misty white, vaporish or have a decidedly human form and appearance (very often with discernible "clothing"), shadow beings are much darker and more shadow-like. In general, although the shadow people often do have a human outline or shape, because they are dark, the details of their appearance are lacking. This is in contrast to many ghost sightings in which the witness can describe the ghost's facial features, style of clothing and other details. The one detail most often noted in some shadow being sightings is their glowing red eyes.

DEMONS OR OTHER SPIRIT ENTITIES

The dark countenance and malevolent feelings that are often reported in association with these creatures has led some researchers to speculate that the Shadow People may be demonic in nature. If they are demons, we have to wonder what their purpose or intent is in letting themselves be seen in this manner. Is it merely to frighten?

Figure 71: Demon skull

The best argument in favor of entity existence can be found in the fact that almost all traditional societies believed in the existence of entities and had developed methods for dealing with them, beginning in ancient times and continuing forth until today.

The basic definition of an entity of spirit is a non-physical energy parasite with some consciousness of its own which attaches to your subtle energy body just as physical parasites do (intestinal worms etc). The level of consciousness held by these beings varies with the individual as does their effect on the human (or animal) host and so the signs of spirit entity attachment are many and varied, ranging from physical aches and pains to paranoid delusion and complete spirit possession.

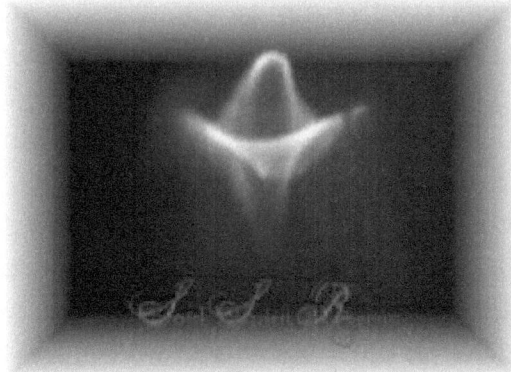

Figure 72: Entity of Spirit

Almost all shamanistic teachings have methods for the clearing of spirits. Ayurveda (traditional Indian medicine) was divided into eight branches, one of which (bhuta-vidya) was devoted to the science of spiritual entities. This places spirit entity clearance in this particular culture at the same level of importance as surgery or pediatrics!

In Chinese medicine in the practice of acupuncture, among the 361 acupuncture points, we see the word KUEI (meaning discarnate spirit) making up part of the main or secondary name of 17 points, thus supporting the Chinese belief in the importance of the spirit in maintaining the health and wellbeing of the body generally.

From the Vedas to the New Testament, there can be found many unambiguous references to the clearance of spirits and entities and many religions have technical rituals dating from ancient times for taking care of the energetic "pollution" arising from someone's passing and work to protect the living from that circumstance.

With this in mind, we can be sure that spirit entities are not simply some kind of odd theory made up to frighten people. If anything it is our modern Western Culture that is at odds with history and all other cultures as it disregards the existence of spirits and entities to the detriment of those people who suffer mentally, emotionally and physically due to attachment.

ASTRAL TRAVELERS

One interesting idea suggests that shadow people are the shadows or essences of people who are having out-of-body experiences. According to ancient eastern teachings, astral projection is a reality. Jerry Gross, an author, lecturer and teacher regarding the principals of astral travel, states that we all travel out of the body when we are asleep.

Figure 73: Astral Traveler

The concept of astral projection has been around for a long time, but until today, it has been hidden from most of humanity. Now, with the aid of astral projection, new levels of knowledge and power enable us to discover the answer to Man's eternal question about life in the physical body. Death takes on a new meaning as we begin to realize that it is only a transition to another dimension, or place of existence. By learning to astral project, we can learn many things about ourselves, and unlearn many things that were previously thought to be true. This leads us to the realization that our physical bodies are only a part of our entire selves, and there is more to our existence than meets the eye! Perhaps, this theory says, we are seeing the ephemeral astral bodies of these twilight travelers.

TIME TRAVELERS

People from our own future, another idea states, could have found the means to travel to the past - our time. However they are able to accomplish this incredible feat, perhaps in that state they appear to us merely as passing shadows as they observe the events of our timeline. "The short answer is that time travel into the future is not only possible, it's been done, and we've known about it for over a century," says Davies. "The reason that the public doesn't seem to know about it is because the amount of time travel

Figure 74: Is Time Travel Possible?

involved is so pitifully small that it doesn't make for a 'Doctor Who' style adventure."

A phenomenon called time dilation is the key here. Time passes more slowly the closer you approach the speed of light -- an unbreakable cosmic speed limit. As such, the hands of a clock in a speeding train would move more slowly than those in a stationary clock. The difference would not be humanly noticeable, but when the train pulled back into the station, the two clocks would be off by billionths of a second. If such a train could attain 99.999 percent light speed, only 1 year would pass onboard for every 223 years back at the train station.

But speed isn't the only factor that affects time. On a much smaller scale, mass also influences time. Time slows down the closer you are to the center of a massive object.

"Time runs a little bit faster in space than it does down on Earth," Davies says. "It runs a little faster on the roof than it does in the basement, and that's a measurable effect."

A clock aboard an orbiting satellite experiences time dilation due to both the speed of its orbit and its greater distance from the center of Earth's gravity.

"Both gravity and speed can give you a means of jumping ahead in time," Davies says. "So in principle, if you had enough money, you could get to the year 3000 in as short a time as you like -- one year, one month, whatever it takes. It is only a question of money and engineering."

INTERDIMENSIONAL BEINGS

Figure 75: Are shadow people interdimensional beings?

Even mainstream science is fairly convinced that there are dimensions other than the three with which we are familiar. And if these other dimensions exist, who or what (if anything) inhabits them? Some theorists say that these dimensions exist parallel and very close to our own, although invisible to us. And if there are inhabitants in these other dimensions, it is possible that they have found a way to intrude on our dimension and become, at least partially, visible? If so, they could very well appear as shadows. It has long been held by psychics and other sensitives that beings on other planes of existence are of different "vibrations." Science is beginning to look at reality, on a quantum level, in the same way that particles of the smallest size exist as vibrations. Perhaps, some theorize, the vibrations of our existence are beginning to mesh with those of another dimension, which accounts for the increase in such phenomena as ghosts, shadow people and possibly aliens.

ALIENS

The alien and abduction phenomena are so bizarre that it's no surprise that extraterrestrials are suspects as the shadow people. Abductees have reported in many cases that the alien grays seem to be able to pass through walls and closed windows, and to appear and disappear abruptly, among other otherworldly talents. Perhaps, too, they can go about their alien agenda disguised in the shadows.

There's a good deal of overlapping among the above ideas, of course. Aliens and ghosts could be interdimensional beings, or aliens could be time travelers - and some believe that the entities that we call demons are responsible for all of these disturbing phenomena.

There is no way to prove or disprove any theories about a phenomenon that is so mysterious, that happens so quickly and without warning. Science finds it virtually impossible to catalog or study such phenomena in any methodical way. All we can do, at present, is to document personal experiences and try to piece together what the shadow people phenomenon might be. It is certainly interesting that we are dealing with a phenomenon that can enter any home at any time and listen in on any conversation. Remember, knowledge is power.

I would also point out that Clark's Law is applicable here. Remember, that law says that any science, advanced enough is indistinguishable from magic. If the gods who once ruled the earth were advanced enough eons ago to have space travel how much more advanced are they today?

Perhaps the mysterious shadow people are simply an old mystery becoming more recognizable or perhaps this mysterious event represents a doorway to and from different planes of existence or perhaps it's just shadows.

CHAPTER ELEVEN
THE MASTERS

There is no doubt that UFOs have been linked with the mysterious Reptilians and the Reptilians have played at being gods on this world for eons. So let us turn our attention back to what we have referred to as the ultimate secret society, the one that seems to generate and control the other societies. What would seem to be their master plan? Well we can get some information on the master plan by studying the reports made by those who claim to have been abducted by UFOs.

ARYAN ABDUCTIONS

Dr. David Jacobs, a professor of history at Temple University in the United States, made a long and detailed study of abductee reports and published his conclusions in a book called *The Threat: The Secret Agenda*[39]. According to Dr. Jacobs, the "alien agenda" includes breeding hybrids

---

[39] Jacobs, David, The Threat: The Secret Agenda, Simon & Schuster, New York. 1988

using human and alien genetic material, and replacing human society with these hybrids which would be under their direct control. This is the real reason behind all the abductions in which male sperm is taken or females are impregnated, according to Dr. Jacobs. He says the first stage is to cross human genetics with the "alien".

It should be considered that this is exactly what the ancient legends say took place eons ago when the "gods" impregnated human females. In fact, such acts are the basis for several major religions. Remember the virgin birth of Jesus, his father being God.

According to both the legends as well as modern scientific research, this genetic material is fused with another human egg and sperm, and this second-stage hybrid is crossed with another human egg and sperm. The result of this would look almost human and when this is crossed with yet another human egg and sperm, the result could walk down the street without being noticed[40]. He could be describing here the way the first creation of the Anunnaki, what some people call "the Adam", was evolved into the human mammal we see today.

Dr. Jacobs also believes that these later-stage hybrids are what abductees call the "Nordics", although not all of them are blond-haired and blue-eyed. The outer appearance does not seem to matter; it is the internal workings that are important. There is also a major difference between the extraterrestrial "Nordics" that came to the Earth and seeded their own bloodlines and the Nordic-type hybrid crossbreeds and others that we might

---

[40] David M. Jacobs, The Threat: The Secret Agenda (Simon and Schuster, New York, 1988), pp 131 and 132

well refer to as Aryans. Dr. Jacobs says that these "super-hybrids" retain many of their "alien" abilities.

Among these "alien" abilities would seem to be the powers to scan the minds of humans and controlling abductees. He suggests that while the hybrids may have some human characteristics, they think like the "aliens" and answer to them. "The hybrid agenda is the alien agenda," he says. Dr. Jacobs believes that in the final stages of the agenda, humans will be slowly "phased out" while the hybrids are "phased in" as the dominate species on the planet.

Memories of loving mothers, fathers, freedom of choice and religion will be replaced by memories of selective breeding, single-minded functions geared to serving the aliens. Dr. Jacobs believes that these hybrids would have a hive mentality with no memories of individual choice, family bonding, or freedom. It would, he says, be a hierarchical, fascist order in which a ruling caste dominates lesser castes. We are almost there, but there is still time to wake up...just.

Dr. Jacobs says that, from interviews with abductees, the hybrids seem unhappy with their situation and long for the same freedoms enjoyed by the humans.

REPTILIAN ABDUCTIONS

As I alluded to earlier, there is more than one group that seems to be struggled for supremacy. There is the alien/hybrid human appearing species and then there also seems to be a reptilian species that is also struggling for control of the planet. There have been numerous stories about them, whether they are called the serpent in the

Garden of Eden or the Dragon or the Djinn in the Middle East they appear to be the same creatures.

Just as the Nordics and the Greys invade bedrooms at night and kidnap unsuspecting people, so to do the Reptilians. In fact, James L. Walden, an American with a doctorate in business education, had so many reptilian experiences that he described them in a book, The Ultimate Alien Agenda[41]. Before his first abduction experiences began, he had no interest in extraterrestrials or UFOs or "science fiction" of any kind. But like many, after his ordeal began, he became very interested in these topics.

His story began in March of 1992 when a grey entity some four feet tall with large dark eyes and a large, bulbous head, appeared in his bedroom just as he was switching off the light to go to bed.

The air became extremely cold and a "petrified" Walden began to cry. He said the right eye of the grey enlarged and turned bright red. It projected a beam of red light, which struck him painfully on the leg. A beam of white light later came down towards him, he said, and it entered his body just below the navel. He lost consciousness and when he woke he was lying on a cold table of polished metal.

He was immobilized and a bright overhead light was shining in his eyes. Around him were people in "stiff white smocks". Some appeared human, but most looked like the being that came to his bedroom. They examined every part of his body and a sperm sample was taken. The Zulu shaman Credo Mutwa describes a similar scene and

---

[41]Walden, James L., The Ultimate Alien Agenda, Llewellyn Publications, St. Paul, Minnesota. 1998.

events during his abduction in what is now Zimbabwe in the early 1960s (see The Reptilian Agenda, part one).

Walden said he was told that he was in an underground facility in south-east Kansas and would not be harmed. He heard a "telepathic voice" say: "You are not who you think you are, and you must accept this." In later experiences, he was told that he was a reptilian-human hybrid.

Many strange things began to happen to him after the first abduction:

"One night...I was lying on my back and searching the ceiling for sleep, when I heard a loud 'whishing' sound. Something moved toward me at lightning-speed -and a large, life-like image of George Washington stopped right in front of my face, touching my nose. I heard a loud, forceful voice, say: *'George Washington was one of us. So are you. You must accept.*[42]'"

George Washington was an Illuminati bloodline, a Grand Master Freemason, and first President of the United States. In the years that followed, James Walden had many other experiences with greys and other more obvious reptilians and worked with the abduction researcher Barbara Bartholic to uncover what was going on. She had heard the same story many times from other people claiming to be abductees.

One entity that Walden experienced was an "interdimensional reptile". It was between eight and twelve feet tall and had elongated feet. There was a "web" between his torso and arms, "like a bat", which could sometimes

---

[42] Ibid

look like wings, and a "fin-like appendage" on his back. His head was large and elongated like a watermelon. The being had rough, greenish patterned skin, and Walden believed there was a tail also. This entity claimed to have inhabited many "human" bodies and he said:

"My eyes have witnessed the evolution of humankind.[43]"

Under hypnosis, Walden recalled that he was part of an experimental group of human embryos, which were grown in a test tube. The embryo, he recalled, was implanted into his mother's womb and she had no idea this had been done. Could this be an explanation of the legends of Merovee, Alexander the Great, and others, who were said to have been fathered by serpent-like beings? And could this be at least one origin of the "Virgin Birth"?

Walden said it certainly offered an explanation for why he had always felt different to all the other children. He believed that millions of people in the world had been created in this way as part of an "alien" genetic program. He said that the semen, taken during his abduction, was used to impregnate a woman of the "same stock". She was like a "human incubator" and he thinks the embryo was removed from her womb later.

Another interesting memory he had was that when he was on the table in that first abduction, his body had looked the same as the "aliens".4 Walden felt that this was another-dimension of him, which inhabited his human form. He believed from his experiences that the "aliens"

---

[43] Ibid

could transcend time, transform matter, manipulate human thought and behavior, and create "distracting illusions to satisfy the needs of our simple human minds."

He concluded that they could move between dimensions and that they were less "extraterrestrial" and more "interdimensional". I thoroughly agree. Their ability to change their vibrational state would explain how they can appear and disappear (leave our frequency range), and how they can walk through walls. They can move through dense matter in the same way a radio frequency can.

And if it is the fourth-dimensional level of a person that is abducted, and not, or not always, the physical body, it would further explain why abductees have described being taken through walls and buildings. Walden speculated that these fourth-dimensional "aliens" are actually the fourth-dimensional level of us.

The abductors told Jim Walden that an interdimensional race had colonized the Earth and they came to harvest the planet's resources, harness its energies, and use primitive humans as its workforce.

"Just as human scientists have developed animals for nourishment, labor, and entertainment purposes," he said, *"alien scientists have improved humans for the same reason - and possibly others."*5

Walden said the "aliens" could program the emotional responses of their hybrids, to produce "misery, jealousy, passion, or love." Walden said that when the interdimensional reptilians first colonized the Earth they found it difficult to reproduce here. He said that during abductions, the "aliens" made it possible for them to inhabit the abductee's body.7

Then there are the experiences of Cathy O'Brien, the mind controlled slave of the United States government for more than 25 years, which she details in her astonishing book, *Trance Formation Of America*[44], written with Mark Phillips. The president of Mexico in the 1980s, Miguel DeLa Madrid; also used Cathy in her mind controlled state. She said he told her the legend of the Iguana and explained that lizard-like extraterrestrials had descended upon the Mayans in Mexico. The Mayan pyramids, their advanced astronomical technology and ~ the sacrifice of virgins, was inspired by lizard-like aliens, he told her."' He added that these reptilians interbred with the Mayans to produce a form of life they could inhabit. De La Madrid told Cathy that these reptile-human bloodlines could, fluctuate between a human and iguana appearance through chameleon-like abilities - "a perfect vehicle for transforming into world leaders", he said. De la Madrid claimed to have Mayan-lizard ancestry in his blood which allowed him to transform back to an iguana at will. He then changed before her eyes, as Bush had, and appeared to have a lizard-like tongue and eyes." Cathy understandably believed this to be another holographic projection, but was it really? Or was De La Madrid saying something very close to the truth? This theme of being like a chameleon is merely another term for 'shape-shifting', a theme you find

---

[44] O'Brien, Cathy and Mark Phillips, Trance Formation of America, Reality Marketing Inc; Revised edition (August 8, 2005)

throughout the ancient world and among open minded people, in the modern one too.

This would explain why Miguel de la Madrid said they needed to create "bodies" through which they could operate on this planet. Walden said the aliens lived in "subterranean shelters" from the time they arrived, and conditions in the Earth's atmosphere threatened their survival because they could not maintain a constant body temperature. He said their eyes are extremely sensitive to light and this fits with Credo Mutwa's claims about the light-sensitive eyes of the greys and other reptilians, and with the symbolic story of the blood-drinking Dracula who could not go out during the day.

Walden was, surprisingly, very positive about the reptilians by the time his book was finished, but I think he was taking their word for their true intentions for humanity a little too easily. The evidence is overwhelming that some of them have a very malevolent agenda, but that is only one large faction, not all of them. Some other abductees also see the reptilians in a positive light, despite having horrendous experiences with them, and some researchers get incredibly angry with anyone who paints the reptilians in a negative light.

REPTILIAN MASTERS

Mark Amaru Pinkham, author of *The Return Of The Serpents Of Wisdom*[45], superbly details the serpent symbolism and bloodlines of the ancient world, but sees them in a virtually 100% positive light. He even praises

---

[45] Pinkham, Mark Amaru, The Return of the Serpents of Wisdom, Adventures Unlimited Press; 1 ED edition (1997).

people like Benjamin Franklin as a force for enlightenment. Franklin sacrificed children! Depicting all reptilians as expressions of "wisdom" is just as ludicrous as depicting them all as "evil". And those who have a horrific agenda for humanity, of course, want us to believe they are here to "save" us.

Stories about people waking up to find reptilian figures in the room are regularly reported. Pamela Hamilton, an American woman who has lived in California and Arizona, claims to have been visited at home, often in the bedroom, by countless "Nordic" blond-haired, blue-eyed beings, along with greys and reptilians, since she was young.8 Witnesses have seen the marks on her body that have followed many of these visits.

She has also suffered a raid by military personnel who walked in and stole material relating to extraterrestrials and UFO activity. Pamela described a reptilian "visitor" who appeared a number of times. She said he had luminous amber-colored eyes like a cat and had grey-green skin and sharp claws on his fingers. He wore a sort of "breast-plate" like the ones used by Roman soldiers, she said.

When he appeared she would first hear a high-pitched sound and a buzzing and clicking noise and soon found it hard to breath. She felt that her chest was being crushed. When she became paralyzed and immobilized, the reptilian would "flip" her on to her chest and begin to have "a type of tantric sexual intercourse" that would leave her exhausted. Feeding on her life force, probably. She said he was extremely powerful and very aggressive and a likely member of a warrior caste. But she didn't fear him and almost felt protected by him.

California and Arizona appear to be extremely important areas for reptilian activity, especially locations such as: Mount Lassen, a dormant volcano that is part of the Cascade Range of California, Oregon, Washington State, and south-western Canada; Sedona, the "New Age" center in Arizona; and Phoenix, two hours south of Sedona in the Valley of the Sun. The Superstition Mountains outside Phoenix have been the subject of a number of stories in which people claim to have seen physical reptilian beings.

One involves a woman known as "Angie" who loved climbing the mountains around Phoenix, including the Superstitions.9 On this occasion she found a cave and went inside. She sat down and began to drink water from her flask. After a while she got up to leave when suddenly she felt a hand grab hers from behind. She gasped in surprise when she looked up at a reptilian face. She tried to laugh, thinking it was someone wearing a mask. When she realized it was for real she tried to scream, but nothing would come.

She lost consciousness and when she awoke she heard strange barking and chirping sounds that she later realized were a sort of "language" the reptilians used. When she tried to get up, she found she couldn't move her arms or legs. She felt a hand on the inside of her thighs and she struggled to open her eyes. She opened one a little and saw men with lizard-like faces. Her heart sank and she felt absolute horror burst through her.

Again when she tried to scream, she couldn't. She watched as several greenish reptilians removed her clothes. They seemed to be a strange combination of human and serpent, she said. The wide slit eyes almost glowed with a yellowish brightness (exactly what Credo Mutwa says), and they had glistening, vertical pupils. They had broad flat noses and their flat nostrils flared slightly as they snorted while examining her. She said that some had a very wide mouth with many folds of skin, while some had small mouths with no folds.

They had small, rounded ears, which were set high on the head, and had no lobes. She noticed that their scales were a different color than the skin on the head. They were a khaki green that became grey-green on the back of the head. Their faces were smooth with narrow, pointed chins. Two of them wore a white jumpsuit with an insignia that included a curved dragon with a seven-pointed star in the middle. The other 'reptile-men' wore black uniforms with the same insignia. She also talked of a tall, white-skinned lizard being with blue eyes -the ones identified many times as the "royal Draco", the highest of the reptilian hierarchy. He wore a "burnt orange jumpsuit" with three insignia on the left side.

There was a black inverted triangle, the round dragon with a star, and an oval with moving stars on it. On the right side of his uniform were three black bars on a silver disk; and the left cuff had a row of inverted triangles with three lines cutting through it. He was taller than the others, nearly seven feet.

Angie was by now naked on the floor and she asked the "white Draco" to help her. She felt something cold touch her forehead, and a strange calm and peace enveloped her. She then realized she was in an oval room about 15 feet wide. She tried to turn her head, but she couldn't. She noticed pipes with strange "sacs", like misshaped balloons hanging from them.

Then she realized some were moving. She remembered how her dog's belly moved that way when she was near full term with her puppies. A wave of horror hit her. It was as if there were two minds inside her. One was calm, the other horror-stricken. The calm side was in charge of her body. She wondered how her body could be so calm when anything could be about to happen to her. One of the lizard men undressed and approached the end of the table. He was muscular and had scales on his chest and lower stomach.

Fear now overwhelmed the artificial calm and she began to scream and find superhuman strength to fight him off. The lizard men turned a blue light on her and she lost consciousness. The last thing she remembered was feeling the weight of his body. When Angie came to, she was in her car. She looked around her, feeling confused and wondering why she was driving her car.

She felt that she had been about to do something, but couldn't remember what. She drove home dazed and disorientated. There she suddenly had an urge to shower, and scrubbed her body for over two hours. She felt shaky and angry for something she couldn't recall. She spent the next few days in bed refusing to answer the door. Her sister Susan noticed that Angie had several nightmares every night and woke up screaming.

Angie also refused to go near the mountains she loved so much. When she later went back to work, she left after three days when a customer brought a lizard into the store. She had no idea why that had frightened her so much when reptiles had always been a part of her life there in the desert. Eventually she went to a hypnotist for help, and her vivid and detailed memories of what happened in the Superstition Mountains flooded back.

Eva Trent, another American, also claims to have had many contacts with nonhuman entities. One night in January 1999, she went to bed in her small apartment. Later, she said, she woke to a "buzzing sound" and when she opened her eyes she was horrified to see two strange creatures standing on either side of her bed. One was around seven to eight feet tall, weighed around 19 stone (getting on for 300 pounds) with the skin of a crocodile or snake. The other was the same, but smaller.

They seemed to be communicating in a "chirping" manner and their eyes glowed. Chirping sounds are pretty common in such reports and the glowing eyes are universal. The Sumerians knew Enlil, the chief Anunnaki on the Earth, as "the Serpent with the shining eyes". Eva found she was unable to move, another confirmation of the ancient and modern accounts of how the serpent "gods" could paralyze people.

They communicated with her through telepathy. She felt they were observing her emotional state and probably feeding off the energy of fear their presence had generated. Similar points were made by Pamela Stonebrooke about the way her reptilian seemed to get high on fear. The experience ended for Eva when she began to mentally resist and visualized herself cocooned in white light.

This seemed to confuse the reptilians and the next thing she remembers was waking up the next morning physically exhausted. When she checked around the room she found five of her favorite cassettes tapes in a rack six feet from her bed had been destroyed. They were distorted and three were badly buckled, as if by some extreme heat. Yet there was no smell of plastic burns and the sound filaments had not been melted. There was no sign of any heat being applied anywhere on or near the rack. The only explanation was that they had been subjected to some kind of microwave heat.

The American writer Alex Christopher has been exposing the reptilian presence for many years and I first saw her speak in Denver in 1996. She is the author of the books, Pandora's Box, volumes I and II, and she has had her own direct experiences of reptilians and the "big-eyed greys". In Panama City, Florida, she was woken at 2.30 in the morning by her terrified neighbor, a commercial airline pilot.

When she ran over to his house, she found his partner sliding down the wall with her eyes rolling and she kept passing out. Alex said she could feel extremely powerful energy in the room, which appeared to be trying to penetrate her head. It was radiation of some kind and the next day all the plants in the room were dead. The couple told her that they were making love when the incident started.

They saw a flash of light and they were pulled from the bed. The man still had a palm print on his side made by fingers that must have been ten inches long with claws that burned into his skin. The next day the spot was so painful he couldn't touch it and Alex says she has video footage of this.

For her, however, the story was just the beginning because when she was in bed in her own house, a reptilian appeared to her:

"I woke up and there is this 'thing' standing over my bed. He had wrap-around-yellow eyes with snake pupils and pointed ears and a grin that wrapped around his head. He had a silvery suit on and this scared the living daylights out of me. I threw the covers over my head and started screaming...I mean, here is this thing with a Cheshire-cat grin and these funky glowing eyes...this is too much. I have seen this kind of being on more than one occasion...He had a hooked nose and was very human looking other than his eyes, and had kind of greying skin...

"...Later on in 1991, I was working in a building in a large city, and I had taken a break about 6pm and the next thing I knew it was 10.30pm and I thought I had taken a short break. I started remembering that I was taken aboard a [spaceship], through four floors of the office building and through a roof.

There on the ship is where I encountered Germans and Americans working together, and also grey aliens, and then we were taken to some other kind of facility and there I saw reptilians again...the ones I call the 'Baby Godzilla's' that have short teeth and yellow slanted-eyes...The things that stick in my minds are the beings that look like reptiles, or the 'velociraptors'. They are the cruelest beings you could ever imagine and they even smell hideous."11

The putrid smell is another theme of contact with reptilians and greys. It was during this abduction that Alex Christopher saw a dragon badge on the uniform of a reptilian. A contact said she saw the same symbol at Fort Walden in the United States and a winged-serpent symbol could be seen on the sleeve of an Israeli soldier as he comforted the daughter of the assassinated Prime Minister, Yitzchak Rabin, during his funeral in 1995 (see Newsweek, November 20th 1995).

Many badges within the US armed forces feature the dragon and reptile, as revealed in the Symbolism Archive on my website. There are many reports of shape-shifting reptilians at military bases and medical facilities. The author and researcher John Keel has gathered together reports of flying reptiles seen by many people. These are known as "pterodactyloid-hominoid moth men", flying serpents, or winged Draco.

These align with ancient and modern descriptions across the world of the "royal" reptilians from the Draco constellation with their wings, tails, and horns. Keel compiled his findings in a book, The Mothman Prophecies (Signet Books, New York, 1976).

Here is a sample:

"...According to her story, Connie [Carpenter], a shy, sensitive eighteen-year-old, was driving home from church at 10:30am on Sunday, November 27, 1966, when, as she passed the deserted greens of Mason County Golf

Course outside New Haven, West Virginia, she suddenly saw a huge grey figure. It was shaped like a man, she said, but much larger. It was at least seven feet tall and very broad. The thing that attracted her attention was not its size, but its eyes. It had, she said, large, round, fiercely glowing red eyes that focused on her with hypnotic effect. 'It's a wonder I didn't run off the road and have a wreck,' she commented later.

"As she slowed, her eyes fixed on the apparition, a pair of wings unfolded from its back. They seemed to have a span of about ten feet. It was definitely not an ordinary bird, but a man-shaped thing, which rose slowly off the ground, straight up like a helicopter, silently. Its wings did not flap in flight. It headed straight toward Connie's car, its horrible eyes fixed to her face, and then it swooped low over her head as she shoved the accelerator to the floorboards in utter hysteria. Over one hundred people would see this bizarre creature that winter."12

Significantly, many of the sightings of these flying reptile-men happened close to the apparently sealed entrances to underground tunnels known as the TNT facility, which were used to store explosives during the Second World War.

A young shoe salesman called Thomas Ury was driving along Route 62 just north of the TNT area when he noticed a tall, grey, man-like figure standing in a field near the road. 'Suddenly it spread a pair of wings', he said, 'and took off straight up, like a helicopter." Native Americans have the legend of the Thunderbird, which, the stories say, abducts children and old people. The tribes of the Dakotas know this as Paisa and it is described as a demon monster with bat wings, a humanoid body, a long tail, and terrifying red eyes. Similar reports have come from many parts of the world.

Another witness called Odette told of an experience at a house in Quebec, Canada. She was with a friend when another woman came over and began to talk about UFOs and contactees. The woman said she was a contactee and she had a meeting with a spaceship on a certain date. She also said that they were taking her and she would never be back on Earth.

Odette said she was not convinced at all and especially when the woman had said that if they could only see her real self, they would see how beautiful she is, like a princess inside.

"I was thinking, yeah right! Whatever!!!", Odette recalled.

The woman looked around 30 years old, tall and strong, light hair, cut to her shoulder, and was "ordinary looking". Then she asked Odette if she would let her reveal her real self because she would never have seen anyone like her. But she said she needed Odette's permission for this. Odette said yes because she thought, "Poor thing, she's really miserable..."

The account continues:

"We went to a quiet room. We sat facing each other, and she grabbed my hands, told me to relax and just look at her. What I saw was a reptile, taller than she was, at least 6 feet, green/brown color, staring at me with its head turned sideways, and I swear with something that seemed like a grin on its face. Then she/it asked me "Didn't I tell you I was beautiful?' I said yes, and headed for the door...If anybody has had a similar experience or knows of a book that talks about reptilians please let me know."13

Men in Black

Reports of reptilian shape-shifters come in from all over the world and the "Men in Black" phenomenon has also been connected to them and the Men In Black have always been connected to UFOs. These are the guys dressed in black suits, who intimidate many UFO researchers and abductees. Most appear to be government agents, but there are other expressions of them who do not look "human" in the usual sense.

They have a strange aura around them and, many people have reported, they can suddenly "disappear". I remember seeing a garage owner and UFO investigator telling his story on a TV program about Men in Black or "MIBs". They turned up out of nowhere without a vehicle and yet his garage was in the middle of the countryside, all by itself. After their conversation, they just as quickly vanished and it was impossible for them to do so under normal circumstances because you could see for miles in all directions.

The Men in Black are named after their dark clothing, mostly business or "agent" suits, and their dark glasses. This attire has all the signs of these beings needing protection from the Sun -a classic trait of the reptilians and greys. They are mostly described as having very white skin and, sometimes, olive skin. The texture is often said to be reptilian. Other strange traits in witness accounts are the trouble the MIBs appear to have breathing and the horrible smell, like sulphur, which abductees are constantly describing.

They also often arrive in "new" black cars that have not been manufactured for decades. Despite their apparent age, these vehicles show no signs of any wear or tear. It is as if they have just been driven from the factory. Similar beings, dressed in the context of the period, have been reported over the centuries in many parts of the world. The so-called Grim Reaper, who appeared in communities just before a lethal disease broke out, were described in terms that are remarkably close to today's Men in Black.

The Association of Extraterrestrial Investigations (APEX), founded by Dr. Max Berezowsky in Sao Paulo, Brazil, documented a Men in Black story involving a young guy called Aeromar[46].14 He said he was harassed by three men dressed in black suits and ties and he thought they were the police. He moved cities twice to get away from them and on one occasion complained to the police in Rio de Janeiro about their harassment.

They didn't believe him and he moved to Sao Paulo. It was there that a car stopped beside him in the street. He said he "lost his will to resist" and climbed inside to find

---

46

the three guys who had been following him for months. He was driven to a wooden area, he said, where he saw a large "UFO". The car stopped and they all walked up to the craft, which was hovering above the ground and surrounded by a "luminous ring".

The next thing he knew, they were inside and he was sat in a chair with handles that secured his wrists. An iron bar pressed his head backwards against the chair and his neck was also fastened. Now, he said, the "Men in Black" transformed. Their "heads ripped open into a heart shape" and their skin became scaled and green like a reptilian.

This happened in 1979-80 long before MIBs became associated with reptilians. He said he also saw human corpses hanging from hooks. Everything went blank after that and he found himself back in the street where he was picked up. Now, however, it was hours later and there was no traffic. He ran home in a panic, he said, and told a roommate what had happened, but as he did so, a force threw him against a wall. The reptilians had told him never to talk about his experience. He was later introduced to Dr. Max Berezowsky and he told his story to APEX members.

On the superb US radio show, Sightings, a woman called Joyce Murphy talked about the reptilian shape-shifters of Brazil. She is the president and founder of Beyond Boundaries, an organization that takes people on expeditions to many parts of the world. She was telling presenter Jeff Rense about some of the strange experiences on her travels when she talked about a policewoman she knew in Brazil who had described shape-shifting reptilian beings.

Joyce said:

"...she works in a very high position in the Sheriff's Office. There seem to be shapeshifters, here in Brazil at least, that try and get women to act as breeders for them. They actually shape-shifted to show them their actual form, a sort of reptilian type. This with her sister as a witness. And I know of another shape-shifter story.

The daughter of an aviation engineer in Sao Paulo tells of a fellow student who revealed her true form changing...into a sort of reptilian being. These people do not know each other and they clam up if one goes after more information or wants to reveal the whole situation. Oh my gosh, what am I getting into here?"15

The Reptilian Underground Bases

There are so many reports of seeing reptilians and shape-shifting, but most people have no knowledge of this because 99% of the population gets their "news" and "information" from the mainstream media. The media, in turn, get their "news" and "information" overwhelmingly from official sources, which, like the media itself, are owned by the reptilian bloodlines. After speaking about the reptilians on the Sightings program, I was sent this account of an experience at the infamous Dulce underground facility in New Mexico.

These are the words of an army private employed on the surface:

"...I was working on a routine job when another of the young enlistees, a mechanic, came in with a small rush job he wanted at once. He had the print and proceeded to show me exactly what he wanted. We are both bending over the bench in front of the welder when I happened to look directly into his face. It seemed to suddenly become covered in a semi-transparent film or cloud. His features faded and in their place appeared a 'thing' with bulging eyes, no hair, and scales for skin."

He later saw the same thing happen to a guard at the Dulce front gate, and witnesses have spoken of seeing reptilian shape-shifters at the Madigan Military Hospital near Fort Lewis in Washington State. There are secret underground facilities throughout the world and at the deepest levels they open out into the inner-earth centers of the reptilians and greys.

Area 51 in Nevada is the best-known underground facility in UFO research circles, but the very fact that it is so famous and featured in Hollywood movies, shows that it is far from the most important of them. These facilities are themselves connected by a vast tunnel network that has been built with nuclear boring technology that the public never sees. It can cut tunnels at the rate of seven miles a day and these are an expansion of the global tunnel network created by the Atlanteans and Lemurians, and claimed by legends and accounts to exist under the United States,

Central and South America, Britain, Egypt, Mesopotamia, Turkey, Asia, China, Malta, everywhere.

The tunnels have state-of-the-art transport systems that move at astonishing speeds. Insiders describe them as "magneto-leviton or mag-lev monorail trains capable of mach-2". Leading Illuminati companies and operations are involved in the construction. Companies like the Rand Corporation, General Electric, AT & T, Hughes Aircraft, Northrop Corporation, Sandia Corporation, Stanford Research Institute, Walsh Construction, the Colorado School of Mines, and the most significant one of all, Bechtel (Beck-tul), a major reptilian corporation.

These underground bases, tunnel systems, and their technology, have been detailed by former military personnel, mind-controlled slaves, and people like Phil Schneider, who helped to build some of them. Schneider was the son of a German U-boat commander in the Second World War, Otto Oscar Schneider. His father was captured and taken to the United States to work for the Illuminati.

As so often happens, the children of Illuminati operatives are brought up to work for the same masters and Phil Schneider says he was commissioned to build sections of a number of underground facilities in the United States. He said he knew of 131 underground military bases, an average of one mile deep, constructed for the New World Order agenda. Two of the bases he was involved with were Area 51 in Nevada and Dulce, New Mexico. Dulce is a small town of around 1,000 people and located on the Jicarilla Apache Reservation at a height of some 7,000 feet.

From in and around Dulce has come a stream of reports of UFO sightings and landings, "alien" abductions, human and animal mutilations, and sightings of reptilians. The base was also the alleged scene, in 1979, of the "Dulce Wars" when reptilians and greys are said to have battled with human military and civilian personnel. Many people on both sides were killed and Phil Schneider claims to have taken part in this shoot-out. He said he was hit by a laser weapon and he had a fantastic scar down his chest, as he publicly revealed.

Schneider talked of his part in the battle in a lecture in 1995, although there appear to be many other elements to it, also:

"My job was to go down the holes and check the rock samples, and recommend the explosive to deal with the particular rock. As I was headed down there, we found ourselves amidst a large cavern that was full of outer-space aliens, otherwise known as large Greys. I shot two of them. At that time, there were 30 people down there. About 40 more came down after this started, and all of them got killed. We had surprised a whole underground base of existing aliens. Later, we found out that they had been living on our planet for a long time. ...This could explain a lot of what is behind the theory of ancient astronauts."

Schneider began to speak out and alert the world to what was going on, although as usual most people didn't listen. Schneider, who worked closely with researcher Alex Christopher, died in January 1996 in highly suspicious circumstances that were crudely made to look like suicide.

Schneider, speaking at a public lecture a year earlier, said:

"...for every calendar year that transpires, military technology increases about 44.5 years [compared with the increase rate of 'conventional' technology]. This is why it is easy to understand that back in 1943 they were able to create, through the use of vacuum tube technology, a ship that could literally disappear from one place and appear in another place."

This was a reference to the "Philadelphia Experiment" in which a US naval ship is alleged to have been made invisible and taken into another dimension. Another of the underground bases Schneider helped to build is under the new Denver International Airport, east of Denver. The construction was very controversial because of the massive cost overrun -the same as the gigantic hole being dug by Bechtel as part of "transport improvements" in Boston, Massachusetts.

Denver Airport is the place with the gargoyles, Freemasonic symbols, and murals full of Illuminati symbolism. I have been through there myself a number of times. According to Schneider, there are several main levels underneath, at least ten sublevels, a 4.5-square-mile underground city, and an 88.5-square-mile underground base. The Denver base is said to include massive "containment camps" and fenced in areas deep underground for holding "dissidents".

Workers who experienced the deeper levels of the base saw scenes so terrifying they have refused to talk about them. From other sources, however, we can imagine some of what they saw. These bases are where many of the millions, yes millions, of children who go missing every year worldwide are taken. I know it is hard to stomach, but they are used for slave labor and eaten by the reptilians, just like humans eat chicken or cows.

Workers at the Dulce base in New Mexico have reported seeing the most grotesque sights in the lower levels. Researchers Bill Hamilton and TAL Levesque (also known as Jason Bishop III) gathered the following information about Dulce, which they published in UFO magazine:

"Level number six is privately called 'Nightmare Hall'. It holds the Genetic Labs. Reports from workers who have seen bizarre experimentation are as follows: 'I have seen multi-legged "humans" that look like half-human/half octopus. Also reptilian-humans and furry creatures that have hands like humans and cry like a baby. It mimics human words...also a huge mixture of lizard-humans in cages. There are fish, seals, birds and mice that can hardly be considered those species. There are several cages (and vats) of winged humanoids, grotesque bat-like creatures...but three and a half to seven feet tall. Gargoyle-like beings and Draco reptoids.

"Level number seven is worse, row after row of thousands of humans and human mixtures in cold storage. Here, too, are embryo storage vats of humanoids in various stages of development. [One worker said] '...I frequently encountered humans in cages, usually dazed or drugged, but sometimes they cried and begged for help. We were told they were hopelessly insane, and involved in high-risk drug tests to cure insanity. We were told never to try to speak to them at all. At the beginning we believed that story. Finally, in 1978, a small group of workers discovered the truth'..."16

This discovery led to the "Dulce Wars", the battle between humans and the reptilians and reptilian greys in 1979 when many scientists and military personnel were killed, and Phil Schneider says he was critically wounded.

A security officer at Dulce called Thomas Castello has described to researchers what happens at the Dulce base and his words were reported in the UFO magazine article. His information has also been circulated as the "Dulce Papers". Castello worked for seven years with the Rand Corporation, an Illuminati operation in Santa Monica, California, and transferred to Duke in 1977.

He estimated there were more than 18,000 of the "short greys" at Dulce, and he had also seen tall reptilian humanoids. He knew of seven levels, but there could have been more, and he said the "aliens" were on levels five, six, and seven. The lower you go, the higher the security clearance you need. The only sign in English was above the tube shuttle station which said "to Los Alamos", another major underground reptilian base in New Mexico. Most signs at Dulce are in the "alien symbol language" and a universal symbol system understood by humans and aliens, he said.

The Illuminati communicate above ground in the language of symbolism, as revealed in The Biggest Secret and the Symbolism Archive on my website. The hieroglyphics of Sumer, Egypt, and China, would have been a reptilian or "alien" language originally. Other tunnel connections from Dulce went to underground facilities at Page, Arizona, Area 51 in Nevada, Taos, Carlsbad, and Datil, New Mexico, Colorado Springs and Creede, Colorado. Castello said there was a vast network of tube shuttle connections under the United States, which extends into a global system of tunnels and sub-cities.

He described the immense security at Dulce. Below the second level, everyone is weighed naked and given a uniform. Any change in weight is noted and people are examined and X-rayed if there is a change of three pounds.

At the entrance to all "sensitive" areas there are scales and a person's weight must match with their card and code to gain entry. Castello also revealed some of the genetic work carried out at Dulce. He said that their scientists can separate the "bioplasmic body" from the physical body and place an "alien entity" (consciousness) within a human body after removing the "soul" of the human. I have thought for years that some famous people, including prime ministers and presidents, were taken into such facilities and possessed by a reptilian entity.

To the public the famous person looks the same physically afterwards, but now a very different force is deciding the behavior. Ancient legends also tell of people being replaced in the night by "changelings" or shape-shifters. It is likely that certain bloodlines with a threshold ratio of reptilian DNA makes this possession easier and this is one reason why the Illuminati keep such detailed genetic records of family bloodlines.

The joint global press announcement by the Illuminati's Bill Clinton and Tony Blair in 2000 about the mapping of the human genome takes on even greater significance when you think that the US Department of Energy has laboratories at Dulce and is closely connected to the genome project, along with the National Institute of Health, the National Science Foundation, and the Howard Hughes Medical Institute. All are Illuminati fronts.

Researcher Alan Walton, who writes extensively on the Internet about the reptilian connection, says:

"Underneath most major cities, especially in the USA in fact, there exist subterranean counterpart 'cities' controlled by the Masonic/hybrid/alien 'elite'. Often surface/ subsurface terminals exist beneath Masonic Lodges, police stations, airports, and federal buildings of major cities ... and even not so 'major' cities. The population ratio is probably close to 10% of the population (the hybrid military-industrial fraternity 'elite' living below ground as opposed to the 90% living above). This does not include the full-blood reptilian species who live in even deeper recesses of the Earth.

"Some of the major population centers were deliberately established by the Masonic/hybrid elite of the Old and New 'worlds' to afford easy access to already existing underground levels, some of which are thousands of years old. Considering that the Los Alamos Labs [in

New Mexico] had a working prototype nuclear powered thermol-bore drill that could literally melt tunnels through the Earth at a rate of 8 mph 40 years ago, you can imagine how extensive these underground systems have become.

These sub-cities also offer close access to organized criminal syndicates, which operate on the surface. They have developed a whole science of 'borgonomics' through which they literally nickle-and-dime us into slavery via multi-leveled taxation, inflation, sublimation, manipulation, regulation, fines, fees, licenses... and the entire debt-credit scam which is run by the Federal Reserve and Wall Street.

"New York City, I can confirm, is one of the largest draconian nests in the world. Or rather the ancient underground 'Atlantean' systems that network beneath that area. They literally control the entire Wall Street pyramid from below... with more than a little help from reptilian bloodlines like the Rockefellers, etc. In fact these reptilian genetic lines operate in a parasitic manner, the underground society acting as the 'parasite' society and the surface society operating as the 'host' society. ...As for the New York City / Wall Street 'nest', during the bombing of the World Trade Center (aka World Slave Center) wherein terrorists attempted to topple one of the towers into the other, a little known fact was briefly revealed.

A six-level sub-basement controlled by the US Secret Service suffered heavy damage. These six sub-basements, one beneath the other, may not have ended there, based on other information that I've uncovered of massive alien infestation beneath the New York City area. These subbasements may actually serve as a major terminal between the underground society of Masonic elite, and the surface society which it controls."

I am sure that the locations of these major cities were selected because they were above underground reptilian-Nephilim tunnel and cavern systems and/or they were on significant vortex points. Phoenix, Arizona, is built on one of these ancient networks, as is Los Angeles -the city of the "angels".

Lauren Savage, the Webmaster of davidicke.com in Texas, says that every county in that state has a building with gothic European architecture (i.e. reptilian), which could not normally have been afforded by Texas when these settlements were built in the 1870's. Many have gargoyles. These buildings, he says, are the county courthouses sitting above underground tunnels and basement systems.

Dallas is an example with its underground tunnels beneath Dealey Plaza where President Kennedy was shot in 1963. What a great way for the true assassins to escape. These tunnels would have been under the original Masonic lodge in Dallas, which was located in Dealey Plaza. Close by is the 1870's old red courthouse complete with gargoyles. Underground tunnels were discovered in Dallas in the late 50's or early 60's and Lauren talked to a man who was working on a state road crew when he was a teenager.

They were digging out what is called "the canyon" to build freeways when they opened up an ancient tunnel. They found rail-type tracks and a sort of train with no known source of fuel or energy. They followed the tunnel to where it ended or collapsed, under an old livery stable. Dallas was a French settlement, earlier called Arcadia (an Illuminati code relating to Atlantis), and a suburb is still named Arcadia Park. In 1999, they revealed that the Capitol building in Austin has underground facilities, which they were going to restore. This building was the headquarters of George W. Bush before he was manipulated into the presidency.

Alan Walton says that Thomas Castello, the Dulce security director, described how the greys, "reptilians", and winged "mothmen" collaborate in the lower levels of the underground system, which includes Dulce and Los Alamos. The command pyramid, he says, seems to be moth men, reptilians, and greys, with the hybrids and humans under them.

Castello also says that one of the reptilians told him that the surface of the Earth was their original home before they were removed in a war the war of the gods -in far ancient times. They escaped underground, to other stars and planets, and even into the fourth and fifth dimensions, Castello says he was told. This fits with the accounts of Credo Mutwa and many abductees who have told of how the reptilians evolved on this planet and were overpowered by other extraterrestrial groups, especially the Nordics.

A woman known as "D" claims to have seen the underground facilities at China Lake Naval Weapons

Centre in the California Desert, one of the major mind control centers of North America. It straddles a vast area and very little can be seen above ground. I have driven around the outside of the base twice now. On one side the public road runs alongside the perimeter fence for a while.

The entrance to China Lake is in the little town of Ridgecrest and this is where "D" once lived. Ridgecrest is home to many mind-controlled slaves programmed at China Lake and it's not far from where the mass murderer Charles Manson and his "Family" used to live. "D", a victim of trauma-based mind control, said that the military chose her because of her bloodline. They had told her that before the development of language, humans communicated by telepathy thanks to a hormone secreted in the brain.

This hormone, she was told, was no longer operating in most people, only in particular bloodlines, including hers, and they wanted to use these abilities. The period, thousands of years ago, when this telepathic human brain function was genetically suppressed was almost certainly symbolized by the story common to most ancient cultures of the gods giving people different languages to divide them and stop them communicating.

"D" said she was taken underground at China Lake and saw the genetics laboratory and holding center for captured humans and genetically engineered mutants. (The true symbolism of the Mutant Ninja Turtles who lived underground in "sewer" tunnels and came out to "fight evil"?) Reptilian symbolism, most of it painting reptilians in a very positive light, has been bombarding the minds of children in recent years.

"D" described seeing horrendous creatures of all types, shapes, and sizes at China Lake. She said she was shown these horrors to let her see what would happen to her if she did not co-operate and she claimed her own son had been murdered. Under China Lake, she said, a reptilian sexually assaulted her and she saw another cut open the chest of a grey. "D" confirmed from her experience that the greys are terrified of the reptilian leadership and do whatever they tell them.

On another occasion, she said, she was taken to the reptilian base under the appropriately named Death Valley, a relatively short drive from China Lake. There she said she saw a reptilian leader, much taller than the others, who was wearing an Egyptian headdress with a cobra snake motif.

The respected UFO researcher, Timothy Good, quotes two "high-placed sources" in his book, Unearthly Disclosure, who confirm the existence of underground extraterrestrial bases. One was from the US Air Force and the other from the US Navy. The reliability of these sources was supported by Admiral of the Fleet, Lord Hill-Norton, the former chief of the UK Defense Staff and former chairman of the NATO Military Committee.

Good says that the sources provided evidence that the American military was working with unidentified "aliens" who have established bases on the planet.19' Many of these bases were underwater, Good was told, a fact that would fit with the ancient legends of the "gods" emerging from the water. The sources said that bases exist in Australia, the Pacific Ocean, the former Soviet Union, the United States, and the Caribbean.

The latter is believed to be in Puerto Rico. The US air force contact told Good: "They [the "aliens"] are here on a permanent basis. They are after this planet." He also said they were "messing with plate tectonics", the movement of land that causes earthquakes, and that the warming of the world's oceans was connected to extraterrestrial activity20 Well it isn't global warming, that's for sure.

Interestingly, Good's sources suggested that the "aliens" were involved in "hybridization" experiments to allow their race to take over the planet... This, however, began a long, long, time ago.

T'was always so

The stories of reptilians and other non-human races living within the Earth in what we would today call "bases", cities, or tunnel networks, can be found widely described in ancient accounts also. The Nagas, or serpent people, in India and throughout Asia and the Far East, were said to live in two main underground centers called Patala and Bhogavati.

From there, according to Hindu legend, they battle for power with the Nordic underground kingdoms of Agharta and Shambala. Hindus believe that Patala can be entered at the Well of Sheshna in Benares, while Bhogavati is believed to be in the Himalayas. Similar stories of underground caverns and tunnel systems can be found in Tibet and China. In the Gilgamesh stories of the Sumerian tablets, we are told of vast underground cities.

Gilgamesh was a "demi-god" and "semi-divine" (reptilian hybrid) who sought the immortality of the "gods". The stories speak of KI-GAL or "the Great Below", which was ruled by the goddess Ereshkigal and the god Mergal. In the KI-GAL were violent guardians called "scorpion men", reanimated human bodies, spirits and the "undead", and robotic beings known as Galatur or Gala, which were used to abduct humans from the surface.

There were "eagle-headed" reptilians, which were often said to have wings. The accounts describe a race called the Pazazu, a dog-faced "human" with reptilian scales and tail. All this sounds remarkably like the scenes described at Dulce today. Chinese legend claims that an underground world entered from the Eastern Mountain of Taishan was guarded by vicious demons called Men Shen with animal-like faces or masks.

This was the Chinese "Hell" and it is said that the Lords of Hell interacted with the Dragon Kings on the surface. The Japanese "Hell" or underground network was similar, and among the non-human entities were the Kappa, semi-aquatic reptilian humanoids and other shape-shifters who lived in mountains, under the ground, or under the sea.

In Viking-Norse legend they have the giant serpent, Nidhoggr or Jormungand, that lived underground and this was similar to the giant serpent Apophis in Egyptian myth. The Scandinavians and Germans had their Huldre or "Hidden Folk" who were also known as the elves. One of the codes for the bloodline is "elven" and the beings of folklore like trolls, etins, fairies, elves, troglodytes, Nephilim, Brownies or Braunies, and the "little people" of Ireland are all different names for the subterranean entities described in the modern accounts of "ET bases".21

All the same stories are associated with them - interbreeding with humans, unable to go out in the sunlight, and all the rest. They even mention the "missing time" experience of people abducted by the "fairies" and include many stories of these underground folk killing and mutilating cattle and taking the blood. Michael Mott has produced an excellent collection of these stories on underground dwellers in folklore and myth.

His book is called Caverns, Cauldrons, And Concealed Creatures, and is available through my website. He writes that England, Scotland, Wales, and Ireland all have endless traditions of underground peoples with many similarities and common origins between them. It seems to me that Scotland, Ireland, and the British Isles in general are such a major center for the Illuminati bloodlines because of the number of entrances to the underground world there are in that region. It is the same with other parts of the world like France, Germany, and the Caucasus Mountains.

What is really under the Windsors' Balmoral Castle or the Queen Mother's Glamis Castle in Scotland, that key country for Illuminati bloodlines? Interestingly, there is a legendary "secret room" at Glamis. According to a guest, the writer, Sir Walter Scott, and others, it is the family's law or custom that the secret is known to only three people at one time.

They take a "terrible oath" not to reveal the secret. Another guest, Lord Halifax, said that in 1875 a workman at the castle came across a door leading to a long passageway. The man investigated, but then he saw something that made him run back in terror. When the 13th Earl of Strathmore was told what the workman had seen he persuaded him to accept money to emigrate and give his word never to reveal what he saw. Lord Halifax said that after the incident the Earl was a changed man, who became silent and moody, with an "anxious, scared face".

The Norse/Germanic fairies, goblins, trows, knockers, brownies, leprechauns, sidhe (shee), tylwyth teg (terlooeth teig) and so on were either malevolent or indifferent to humanity, Michael Mott says. They lived, virtually without exception, under the ground. Mounds, hills, ruins, ancient raths or hill-forts, mountains, cliffs, and ancient cities were said to be the "rooftops" of their palaces.

Beings that mirror modern reports of the Sasquatch (Big Foot) and the Yeti (Abominable Snowman) can also be found in ancient stories of underground creatures that come to the surface. Like the Nagas, the serpent people of Asia, European folklore often claimed that these "fairy" people entered their underground homes through lakes.

Michael Mott continues:

"To remove all doubt as to their relationship with Norse hidden-folk and Indian Nagas alike, they shunned the sunlight, and often seemed interested in crossbreeding their own bloodlines with those of human beings, or even in crossbreeding their 'livestock' or fairy cattle, horses, hounds and so forth with the surface species which were most compatible. The goblin-dwarf, Rumplestiltskin, in his lust to have the human baby and its genetic bounty, is just one example of this in folklore.

The elves took a regular interest in human affairs- weddings, births, and deaths, (bloodlines), the success of crops and livestock, and so forth -but only for their own selfish interests. They seemed to be overly-concerned with genetic and biological diversity, and they pilfered livestock, crops, and human genes via theft or cross-species liaison whenever they saw fit to do so. The elves are generally depicted as extremely fair-haired and fair-skinned."22

What Mott is describing there from European folklore could have come straight from the mouth of a modern abductee or researcher of the underground bases. The so-called greys of modern UFO legend appear to be the same as the beings known as the Galatur and Ushabtiu who abducted humans from underground in Sumerian and Egyptian myths, and the folklore of the Shetland Islands off the north of Scotland referred to the "little men" who abducted humans as "grey neighbors" and the greys.

In the Americas you find the same legends and accounts of the underground people. They include humans, reptilians, reptilian humanoids, and various "monsters" and "demons". Their descriptions match those of other ancient cultures all over the world. Many Native American tribes, like the Hopi, claim to have lived within these underground cavern "cities" before coming to settle on the surface.

In the Mayan epic, the Popol Vul, two "semi-divine" (hybrid) brothers, Hunapuh and Xbalanque, enter the horrific underground world called Xibalba to battle a crocodile-headed monster and, as a result of their victory, the brothers brought an end to human sacrifice -the calling card of the reptilians to this day. These underground worlds are the origin of the belief in Hell being under the Earth. The poet, Dante (1265-1321), was an initiate of the Knights Templar. In his famous work, the Inferno, he is taken on a tour of the underworld. He says it consisted of ten levels where "sinners" are imprisoned and punished by horned demons and reptilian, bird-like giants called the harpies.

The conditions and environment he describes in this "Hell" can be found in descriptions of these underground worlds and cavern communities everywhere. The accounts even include the idea of being imprisoned down there waiting for the Day of Judgment.

In Ireland and the Isle of Man, two major locations for Illuminati bloodlines and activity, much of their culture is based on fairy legends and "the little people" who live under the ground. Irish legends tell of the sexual relationships between the ancient Milesians and the Tuatha de Danaan, the Irish "underground gods" who fled into the Earth and settled there. St Patrick, who "removed the snakes from Ireland", is said to have seen one of these underground people, a "fairy woman", coming out of the cave of Cruachan.

When St Patrick asks a Milesian about her, he replies:

"She is of the Tuatha de Danaan who are unfading...and I am of the sons of Mil [human Irish], who are perishable and fade away."

The usual tale of mortality and immortality. As Michael Mott reports, Daniel Bradley and other geneticists at the Trinity College in Dublin have discovered that the oldest "pure" racial bloodline in Europe continues to exist in the far west of Ireland.

This, as I highlight in The Biggest Secret, is also the last bastion of an ancient Irish language called Gaelic, which is astonishingly similar to languages of North Africa, such as Libyan. Bradley told the Reuters news agency in March 2000 that the Irish came from a race that was different to other Europeans. He said: "When you look at this old genetic geography of Ireland what you find is that in the west (of Ireland) we are almost exclusively of one type of Y chromosome."

They found that 98% of men with Gaelic names in western Ireland had this particular chromosome. If anyone is still in doubt that the legends of the "fairy" people and the "extraterrestrial" accounts of today are describing the same entities, Michael Mott summarizes here the common attributes of the underground peoples of global folklore:

"They are mostly reptilian or reptilian humanoids or "fair" and Nordic; they are telepathic with superior mental powers; they can shape-shift and create illusions; they want to interbreed with humans and need human blood, flesh, and reproductive materials; they have advanced technology; they have the secret of immortality; they can fly, either by themselves or with their technology; they mostly have a malevolent agenda for humans; they cannot survive for long in direct sunlight; they have been banished from the surface world or are in hiding from surface people and/or the Sun; they want to keep their treasures, knowledge, and true identity a secret; they covertly manipulate events on the surface world; they have surface humans working for them through the priesthoods, cults, and secret societies; they have a putrid smell like "sulphur and brimstone".

The accounts are incredibly consistent over thousands of years.

Mott writes:

"The reptilian aspect of some underworlders permeates folklore. One universal theme that recurs in the folktales of many, many cultures is that of the snake-husband or snake-wife, who can transform into a "human" or humanoid form and is invariably (of course) of royal blood among his or her own kind (talk about the ultimate pick-up line!). Often the snake or serpent-man exacts a promise of marriage, or the hand of an unborn human child in betrothal, consistent with the theme of the subterranean's interest in maintaining their own genetic diversity.
"A variant of this should be familiar to most readers of fairy tales, in the form of 'The Frog Prince'. The frog-prince is a Handsome Prince, but like the Japanese seducing dragon, he has a reptilian or amphibian form. The underworld link is complete, for frequently the frog lives in a deep well, from which he is discovered or rescued by the female protagonist.
A possible connection is evident in the Scandinavian belief that some dwarves would 'turn into toads", if caught by the Sun, much like Mimoto's lover turned from a man into a 'dragon' when the same thing happened. Slovenia has its legends of fairies and 'little people', but Slovenian fairy tales are also permeated by the

presence of the 'Snake Queen', a great, white, cave-dwelling creature who is part woman and part serpent. The serpentine-yet-human Nagas are still believed by devout Hindus and some Buddhists to dwell beneath India, Nepal, and Tibet."23

Denying the obvious

When you read and hear the horrendous accounts of the victims and witnesses of the grotesque reptilian agenda, ancient and modern, it is hard to comprehend how so many "researchers" and New Agers continue to believe that this "extraterrestrial" presence is good for humanity and a sign of positive change. Now, of course, not all "extraterrestrials" or interdimensionals are malevolent, but does that mean that we have to ignore the fact that some of them are?

I have had "researchers" attack me who appear far more concerned with the effect of my work on the image of reptilians than they are with the horrors being perpetrated on abductees, mind-control victims, and the people of the world in general.

Dr. David Jacobs in his book, The Threat, picks up this point. He calls such people "the Positives":

"Often the New Age Positives band together into almost cult-like groups to defend themselves from their detractors -researchers and abductees who have come to different conclusions about the abduction phenomenon. The Positives reinforce one another's feelings and insulate themselves from the terror of their lives; they become angry when "less enlightened" abduction researchers question their interpretation."24

Certain researchers in England, Las Vegas, and the United States in general come immediately to mind. Dr. Jacobs also names some of the "stars" of extraterrestrial research like John Hunter Gray, Dr. Leo Sprinkle, Dr. Richard Boylan, Joseph Nyman, and Harvard professor, Dr. John Mack, among those who want to put a positive twist on the abductee reports:

"Both Boylan and Mack de-emphasize the effects of the standard abduction procedures. Boylan believes that gynecological and urological procedures take place only with a very small number of abductees and he rarely focuses on them. And although Mack has found nearly the full range of alien physical, mental, and reproductive procedures, he only mentions them in passing while emphasizing what he finds to be spiritually uplifting elements.

The benevolent 'spin' that the Positives (both abductees and researchers) put on the abduction phenomenon is puzzling, given the way most people describe their abductions: being unwillingly taken; being subjected to painful physical procedures (sometimes leaving permanent scars); enduring humiliating and abusive sexual episodes, including unwanted sexual intercourse; living with the fear and anxiety of wondering when they will be abducted again."25

James Bartley, the abductee and researcher of the reptilian connection, is rather more blunt in his appraisal of what he calls "the Muppets" -those who either refuse to see the malevolent nature of the reptilian agenda or actively seek to portray it in a positive light. He says the reason why so many abductees are hopelessly confused about this whole mess is because trigger mechanisms have been programmed into them to keep them from getting at the truth of their experiences.

He says he has witnessed countless times how an abductee will immediately fall asleep the moment the lecturer begins talking about "fear-based" issues. But when he or she attends a lecture by a channeller or some other "light worker" saying positive things about the "aliens", the abductee is bright and attentive, and awake during the whole lecture.

"Falling asleep is just one trigger mechanism," he says.

Another is annoyance or anger at the "fear-based" lecturer or abductee. Likewise an overwhelming compulsion to get up and walk out, to get up and eat, to get up and smoke a cigarette, getting nauseous, a headache etc., etc. In an article challenging the methods of researcher and lecturer, Dr. .Richard Boylan, Bartley goes on:

"Boylan... [promotes]... the ludicrous notion that a woman abductee was merely suffering from spiritual retardation and was mentally incapable of understanding the 'benevolent' nature of the horrific and unwanted experimentation that was being conducted on her...We have worked with countless women who have suffered painful and bloody hemorrhages, sometimes lasting for days, after the 'benevolent ET' doctors had made an unwanted house call.

What, the discerning human must ask, does profuse and painful bleeding have to do with 'spiritual' evolution? The New Age La-Dee-Dahs claim that there is no such thing as Evil or Demons, which makes [them] the butt of endless jokes by Witches, Warlocks and Satanists throughout the world because the latter derive their power from demonic entities.

"By constantly blaming 'the military' and the 'globalist industrialists', the reptilian propagandists condition the abductees into believing that all human institutions are bad and that the only hope one has to reach the... 'next level of consciousness, evolution, and vibratory frequency' et al, is to look to the skies towards the same dark gods who are responsible for their current state of spiritual enslavement.

Never mind that for the most part these 'Globalists and Militarists' are part of the same old fraternal orders, which worship the patriarchal serpent gods and in many cases are hosts for reptilian entities themselves. These hosts and their fellow travelers operate as a Fifth Column here on Earth to set the stage for the return of the Dark Reptilian Gods.

"The so-called UFO Research Community is awash with these 'Muppets'. Even I have to laugh at the irony of it: literal hosts for reptilian entities facilitating abductee support groups, lecturing at so-called 'UFO Conferences' and speaking on the Art-Bell Show [the major "mysteries" radio show in the US]. This is so because of the long term genetic and soul matrix manipulation of the human race."26

How right he is and how fast the human race needs to wake up and grow up. The stories I have featured in this chapter are just a small selection of the reports and personal accounts describing reptilian experiences. If you want to see more, go to the Reptilian Archive on my website, read The Biggest Secret, or watch the Bridge of Love videos with Arizona Wilder, Revelations Of A Mother Goddess, and Credo Mutwa, The Reptilian Agenda, parts one and two.

When you put these modern reports together with their mirrors in the ancient world, it constitutes a library of information that only the most imprisoned of minds could dismiss without further investigation. Much of what we refer to as supernatural would seem the be our interpretation of what we perceive, and as Clarke's Third Law proclaims any science sufficiently advanced will be perceived as magic by those less advanced.

But, given the level of human conditioning, many still will. Especially the media.

CHAPTER TWELVE
UNIDENTIFIED FLYING OBJECTS AND SASQUATCH

Figure 76: Well-known photo of Bigfoot

One creature that tends to be lumped into the topic of the supernatural has always been what many call Bigfoot and others refer to as Sasquatch. This is an ape-like creature (referred to as a cryptid since it is currently a denizen of the field of cryptozoology[47]) that purportedly inhabits the forests of the Pacific Northwest region of North America. Bigfoot is usually described as a large, hairy, bipedal humanoid. The term

---

[47] Cryptozoology means, literally, the study of hidden animals and refers to the search for animals whose existence has not been proven. This includes looking for living examples of animals that are considered extinct, such as dinosaurs; animals whose existence lacks physical evidence but which appear in myths, legends, or are reported, such as Bigfoot and Chupacabra; and wild animals living dramatically outside their normal geographic ranges, such as phantom cats or "ABCs" (an initialism commonly used by cryptozoologists that stands for Alien Big Cats). The animals cryptozoologists study are often referred to as cryptids, a term coined by John Wall in 1983

"sasquatch" is an Anglicized derivative of the Halkomelem word sásq'ets.

Scientists discount the existence of Bigfoot and consider it to be a combination of folklore, misidentification, and hoax rather than a living animal, in part because of the large numbers thought necessary to maintain a breeding population. A few scientists, such as Jane Goodall and Jeffrey Meldrum, have expressed interest and belief in the creature, with Meldrum expressing the opinion that evidence collected of alleged Bigfoot encounters warrants further evaluation and testing. Bigfoot remains one of the more famous examples of a cryptid within cryptozoology, and an enduring legend.

Bigfoot is normally described in reports as a large hairy ape-like creature, in a range of 6–10 feet tall, weighing in excess of 500 pounds, and covered in dark brown or dark reddish hair. Witnesses have described the creature as having large eyes, a pronounced brow ridge, and a large, low-set forehead; the top of the head has been described as rounded and crested, similar to the sagittal crest of the male gorilla. Bigfoot is commonly reported to have a strong, unpleasant smell by those who claim to have encountered it at close range.

The enormous footprints for which it is named have been as large as 24 inches long and 8 inches wide. While most casts taken of Bigfoot prints have five toes — like all known apes — some casts of alleged Bigfoot tracks have had numbers ranging from two to six. Some have also contained claw marks, making it likely that a portion of the print shown on the cast came from known animals such as bears, which have five toes and claws. Some proponents have also claimed that Bigfoot is omnivorous and mainly nocturnal.

History of Bigfoot

Stories of the wild men of the words are found throughout the indigenous population of the Pacific Northwest. The legends existed prior to there being a single name for the creature. These stories differed in their details both regionally and between families in the same community. In fact, similar stories of wild men are found on every continent except Antarctica. Ecologist Robert Michael Pyle argues that most cultures have human-like giants in their folk history: "We have this need for some larger-than-life creature."

Members of the Lummi Tribe[48] tell tales about Ts'emekwes, the local version of Bigfoot. The stories are similar to each other in terms of the general descriptions of Ts'emekwes, but details about the creature's diet and activities differed between the stories of different families.

Some regional versions contained more nefarious creatures. The stiyaha or kwi-kwiyai were a nocturnal race that children were told not to say the names in case the monsters heard and come to carried off a person—sometimes to be killed. In 1847, Paul Kane reported stories told by the native peoples about the skoocooms: a race of cannibalistic wild men living on the peak of Mount St. Helens. The skoocooms appear to have been regarded as supernatural, rather than natural, but the descriptions matched those of Bigfoot.

Less menacing versions such as the one recorded by Reverend Elkanah Walker exist. In 1840, Walker, a Protestant missionary, recorded stories of giants among the Native Americans living in Spokane, Washington. The

---

[48] The Lummi, governed by the Lummi Nation, are a Native American tribe of the Coast Salish ethnolinguistic group in western Washington State in the United States. The Tribe primarily resides on and around the Lummi Indian Reservation, to the west of Bellingham and 20 miles south of the Canadian border, in western Whatcom County.

Indians claimed that these giants lived on and around the peaks of nearby mountains and stole salmon from the fishermen's nets.

Various local legends were compiled by J. W. Burns in a series of Canadian newspaper articles in the 1920s. Each language had its own name for the local version of the creatures. Many names meant something along the lines of "wild man" or "hairy man" although other names described common actions it was said to perform (e.g. eating clams).

It was Burns that coined the term Sasquatch, which is from the Halkomelem sásq'et, and used it in his articles to describe a hypothetical single type of creature reflected in these various stories. Burns' articles popularized both the legend and the new name for the creatures, making it well known in western Canada before it gained popularity in the United States.

Figure 77: Daniel Boone

Frontiersman Daniel Boone reported having shot and killed "a ten-foot, hairy giant he called a Yahoo." Folktale scholar Hugh H. Trotti has argued that Boone's account may have been the inspiration for some of the Bigfoot stories told in North America.

In 1951, Eric Shipton had photographed what he described as a Yeti footprint. This photograph generated considerable attention and the story of the Yeti entered into popular consciousness. The notoriety of ape-men grew over the decade, culminating in 1958 when large footprints were found in Del Norte County, California, by bulldozer operator Gerald Crew.

Sets of large tracks appeared multiple times around a road-construction site in Bluff Creek. After not being taken seriously about what he was seeing, Crew brought in his friend, Bob Titmus, to cast the prints in plaster. The story was published in the Humboldt Times along with a photo of Crew holding one of the casts. Locals had been calling the unseen track-maker "Big Foot" since the late summer, which Humboldt Times columnist Andrew Genzoli shortened to "Bigfoot" in his article. Bigfoot gained international attention when the story was picked up by the Associated Press.

Following the death of Ray Wallace – a local logger – his family attributed the creation of the footprints to him. The wife of Scoop Beal, the editor of the Humboldt Standard, which later combined with the Humboldt Times, in which Genzoli's story had appeared, has stated that her husband was in on the hoax with Wallace.

1958 was a watershed year for not just the Bigfoot story itself but also the culture that surrounds it. The first Bigfoot hunters began following the discovery of footprints at Bluff Creek, California. Within a year, Tom Slick, who had funded searches for Yeti in the Himalayas earlier in the decade, organized searches for Bigfoot in the area around Bluff Creek.

As Bigfoot has become better known and a phenomenon in popular culture, sightings have spread throughout North America. In addition to the Pacific Northwest, the Great Lakes region and the Southeastern United States have had many reports of Bigfoot sightings.

Bigfoot Sightings in North America.

About a third of all reports of Bigfoot sightings are concentrated in the Pacific Northwest, with most of the remaining reports spread throughout the rest of North America. Some Bigfoot advocates, such as cryptozoologist

John Willison Green, have postulated that Bigfoot is a worldwide phenomenon. The most notable reports include:

- 1924: Prospector Albert Ostman claimed to have been abducted by Sasquatch and held captive by the creatures in British Columbia.

- 1924: Fred Beck claimed that he and four other miners were attacked one night in July 1924, by several "ape-men" throwing rocks at their cabin in an area later called Ape Canyon, Washington. Beck said the miners shot and possibly killed at least one of the creatures, precipitating an attack on their cabin, during which the creatures bombarded the cabin with rocks and tried to break in. The supposed incident was widely reported at the time. Beck wrote a book about the alleged event in 1967, in which he argued that the creatures were mystical beings from another dimension, claiming that he had experienced psychic premonitions and visions his entire life of which the ape-men were only one component. Speleologist William Halliday argued in 1983 that the story arose from an incident in which hikers from a nearby camp had thrown rocks into the canyon. There are also local rumors that pranksters harassed the men and planted faked footprints.

- 1941: Jeannie Chapman and her children said they had escaped their home when a 7.5 feet tall Sasquatch approached their residence in Ruby Creek, British Columbia.

- 1958: Bulldozer operator Jerry Crew took to a newspaper office a cast of one of the enormous footprints he and other workers had seen at an isolated work site at Bluff Creek, California. The crew was overseen by Wilbur L. Wallace, brother of Raymond L. Wallace. After Ray Wallace's death, his children came forward with a pair of 16-inch (41 cm) wooden feet, which they said their father had used to fake the Bigfoot tracks in 1958. Wallace is poorly regarded by many Bigfoot proponents. John Napier wrote, "I do not feel impressed with Mr. Wallace's story" regarding having over 15,000 feet (4,600 m) of film showing Bigfoot.

- 1967: Roger Patterson and Robert Gimlin reported that on October 20 they had captured a purported Sasquatch on film at Bluff Creek, California. This came to be known as the Patterson-Gimlin film. Many years later, Bob Heironimus, an acquaintance of Patterson's, said that he had worn an ape costume for the making of the film.

- 2007: On September 16, 2007, hunter Rick Jacobs captured an image of a supposed Sasquatch by using an automatically triggered camera attached to a tree, prompting a spokesperson for the Pennsylvania Game Commission to say that it was likely an image of "a bear with a severe case of mange. The photo was taken near the town of Ridgway, Pennsylvania, in the Allegheny National Forest.

- April, 2012, BBC report included a description by Kentuckian Joy Clay of her encounter with a Bigfoot while in a tent.

Gigantopithecus

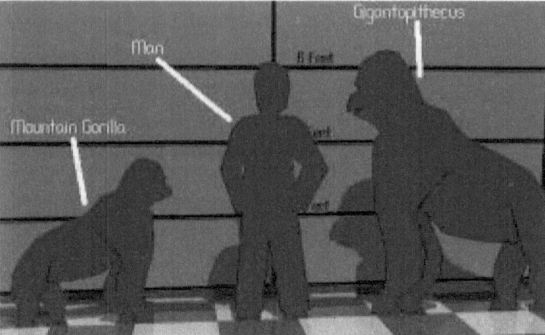

Figure 78: Comparison between Man and Gigantopithecus

Bigfoot proponents Grover Krantz and Geoffrey Bourne believe that Bigfoot could be a relict population of Gigantopithecus. Bourne contends that as most Gigantopithecus fossils are found in China, and as many species of animals migrated across the Bering land bridge, it is not unreasonable to assume that Gigantopithecus might have as well.

The Gigantopithecus hypothesis is generally considered entirely speculative. Gigantopithecus fossils are not found in the Americas. As the only recovered fossils are of mandibles and teeth, there is some uncertainty about Gigantopithecus's locomotion. Krantz has argued, based on his extrapolation of the shape of its mandible, that Gigantopithecus could have been bipedal. However, the relevant part of mandible is not present in any fossils. The mainstream view is that Gigantopithecus was a quadruped, and it has been argued that Gigantopithecus's enormous mass would have made it difficult for it to adopt a bipedal gait.

Matt Cartmill presents another problem with the Gigantopithecus hypothesis: "The trouble with this account is that Gigantopithecus was not a hominid and maybe not even a crown-group hominoid; yet the physical evidence implies that Bigfoot is an upright biped with buttocks and a long, stout, permanently adducted hallux. These are hominid autapomorphies, not found in other mammals or other bipeds. It seems unlikely that Gigantopithecus would have evolved these uniquely hominin traits in parallel."

Bernard G. Campbellin wrote: "That Gigantopithecus is in fact extinct has been questioned by those who believe it survives as the Yeti of the Himalayas and the Sasquatch of the north-west American coast. But the evidence for these creatures is not convincing."

Extinct hominidae

A species of Paranthropus, such as Paranthropus robustus, with its crested skull and bipedal gait, was suggested by primatologist John Napier and anthropologist Gordon Strasenburg as a possible candidate for Bigfoot's identity, despite the fact that fossils of Paranthropus are found only in Africa.

Michael Rugg, of the Bigfoot Discovery Museum, presented a comparison between human, Gigantopithecus and Meganthropus skulls (reconstructions made by Grover Krantz) in episodes 131 and 132 of the Bigfoot Discovery Museum Show. He favorably compares a modern tooth suspected of coming from a Bigfoot to the Meganthropus fossil teeth, noting the worn enamel on the occlusal surface. The Meganthropus fossils originated from Asia, the tooth was found in the Pacific Northwest.

Some suggest Neanderthal, Homo erectus, or Homo heidelbergensis to be the creature, but no remains of any of those species have been found in the Americas.

And So?

So we have a creature which has been a part of legend for centuries which is said to exist in the Pacific Northwest. I do know that there have been sightings as far to the east coast as Chattanooga, Tennessee and northern Georgia which resulted in hard evidence that something unusual was involved. However, as of the time of this writing, there have been no creatures captured nor bodies found. Now we need to see how the UFO becomes involved with this unusual creature.

Involving UFOs

Starting on January 1, 1973, and continuing all year long, reports of strange lights and mysterious aerial objects were being commonly reported across the state of Pennsylvania. The year 1973 was very active in regard to UFO incidents not only in Pennsylvania but also in other states, but events that began to unfold that summer became much more interesting and very unusual. A major outbreak of encounters with Bigfoot creatures was being reported from widespread areas across southwest Pennsylvania as well as other parts of the state. This series of creature encounters went on for months into 1974.

In many cases there were daylight observations where the creatures were observed by witnesses at close range. In other instances, there was more than one creature observed together. As the sightings continued, some of the details of the encounters became much stranger. Among the oddities reported were a number of cases where both a UFO and a Bigfoot were observed at the same time and place. In one case, a UFO was observed on or near the ground and two Bigfoot creatures were observed in the same field. After the object departed and the creatures went into the woods, a state trooper who came to the scene to investigate observed a glowing area on the ground where the object had rested a short time before.

These reports were coming in from the general public from various statewide locations. These cases were also being investigated soon after they occurred, and as unusual as the incidents might have been, they could not be dismissed. It soon became apparent that there were other aspects to the Bigfoot phenomena that could not be ignored.

Luckily for residents, reports of hostility to humans that encountered these creatures have been generally non-existent in the hundreds of Bigfoot cases that have come from the State of Pennsylvania. There is no doubt that they are curious of human behavior and on occasion, have approached quite closely to people engaged in various activities.

There have also been a few cases over the years where these creatures have chased individuals but, even though they could have easily caught them, they did not do so. There have also been some unconfirmed stories, which are rare, of some cases of aggression towards humans, but these incidents sometimes reportedly involved white colored hairy creatures, which are not that often reported.

In Pennsylvania, the typical five toed footprint as well as atypical three toed tracks have been reported and casts were made and they were photographed. The most interesting track that I made a cast of was the three toed footprint found on a hillside behind a house, where something with glowing red eyes had looked into a window eight feet off the ground in 1973. Reports of these types of strange footprints have been a part of Pennsylvania history for many years.

Adding to the mystery have been a number of other strange footprints that have shown up in various statewide locations over many years of tracks unlike the five and three toed variety. For example, some of the tracks were ape-like in appearance. In many of these cases, the tracks and the witness accounts appeared to be credible. This adds even more questions to the Bigfoot phenomena. Over the years various hoax cases were uncovered or in some instances strange tracks were reported that were determined to be normal animal tracks that became distorted in appearance from weather and ground conditions.

A Connection

Most investigators have never given any consideration that UFOs and Bigfoot, might somehow be related. However, listening first hand to the accounts from frightened witnesses sometimes just minutes after their encounters, and finding bits and pieces of evidence at the scene of the events was very convincing.

The eyewitness reports of strange lights or aerial phenomena accompanying the appearance in the same area of a Bigfoot creature from such widespread areas cannot be ignored. Now it is true that most UFO incidents do not involve a Bigfoot creature, and most Bigfoot cases do not have a UFO observation associated with it. Most witnesses that we interviewed had no prior interest in such unusual matters. In some cases those involved asked us why the strange lights and the creatures seemed to show up at about the same time.

There is a small percentage of cases however where observers have seen both a UFO and Bigfoot at the same time and location. From the reports I have received from across the country and around the world, such cases might be much more common, but many researchers have been reluctant to publish such accounts for fear of ridicule from their peers.

You may ask why, if there are so many yearly sightings of these elusive creatures why don't we have more physical evidence or a body as proof. During the 1973 Bigfoot outbreak, many strange incidents came to light which indicated that there may be other aspects to the reality of the Bigfoot phenomena, and as strange as it sounds indicated that at least some of these creatures may not be normal flesh and blood animals. One example was a series of tracks that just suddenly stopped where there should have been more footprints.

Even stranger, there was one case in 1974 that was investigated by the State Police in Fayette County that involved a shooting. A woman fired at a hairy creature with her shot gun that was standing only a few feet away. Instead of falling the creature vanished in a flash of light. At about the same time a luminous object is seen hovering over the nearby woods. No sign of the creature was found after the shooting.

On a farm near Derry, Pennsylvania, there were reports that a Bigfoot kept making repeated appearances as reported by various witnesses. Each time, within minutes after the creature would be seen, strange aerial objects would be observed flying over the property.

In Beaver County, two women watched a white hair covered creature running across a road into the woods carrying a small glowing sphere of light in one hand. Outside of Uniontown, a glowing object lands and two Bigfoot creatures are observed in the pasture at the same time.

Other Research

Researchers such as John Keel and Stan Gordon have noted the apparent parallels between sightings of anthropomorphic ape-like creatures and UFO encounters literally across the country. In some of the smaller Fortean circles, this sort of research has even occasionally led to the suggestion that the Bigfoot creatures might represent some form of an alien being themselves. In fact, various websites have even gone so far as to denote Bigfoot-type creatures under the extraterrestrial classification of "Sasquans" and similar names, likening the beasts to being an extraterrestrial race exiled (whether or not it's a self-imposed exile) here on Earth.

Other bizarre speculation along similar lines suggests that Bigfoot creatures are actually pets which, similar to an irresponsible dog or cat owner taking an animal off to a remote location and release it, have been turned loose on this planet by their extraterrestrial owners.

Other reports seem to denote Bigfoot being used to guard what are said to be the entrances to underground alien bases.

But all the more bizarre speculation put aside, there have actually been studies performed in the past that sought to try and explain why there are, in fact, trends between Bigfoot and UFO sightings. Peter Leeson, a BB&T Professor for the Study of Capitalism at George Mason University, undertook a similar task in 2008. Leeson, who admitted having an interest in UFOs on an economics blog, began plotting UFO sightings on a chart that also tracked Bigfoot sightings graphically.

Even in the early stages, Leeson described "an intriguing pattern," in which he found that states that had more U.F.O. sightings also appeared to be having more Bigfoot sightings. Guest blogging for the New York Times, Leeson wrote that "six of the top ten U.F.O. and Bigfoot states are the same: Washington, Oregon, New Mexico, Alaska, Wyoming, and Colorado. Two states, Washington and Oregon, are among both categories' top five."

Although such information is strange, can we conclude from this that there is indeed a connection between hairy hominids and UFO sightings? Do these Bigfoot creatures, in spite of being purported to look a lot like us, really hailing from someplace further out than we realize? Or, does this information suggest that, in reality, there is a deeper meaning here? What if prevalence of geomagnetic activity were taken into question? Would we be startled to find a propensity for thrust faults and other Earthbound activity conducive to magnetic or electrical phenomena in these states, and if so, could these be factors involved, either in the appearance of these creatures, or at very least, the perception thereof?

CHAPTER THIRTEEN
AND THEN

So there you have it. The evidence that Unidentified flying objects have used what early man has called paranormal abilities in order to manipulate and control humans. Shocking? Certainly it is, but from a tactical stand point it makes sense.

I am sure that there is a hand in the back of the room wanting to point out that mankind is not gullible enough to create major religions around the machinations of visitors from outer space.

That may be true: however, I want to point readers to what is known as the "Cargo Cult." For those who are not familiar with this religion, a cargo cult is a religious practice that has appeared in many traditional pre-industrial tribal societies in the wake of interaction with technologically advanced cultures. The cults focus on obtaining the material wealth (the "cargo") of the advanced culture through magic and religious rituals and practices.

Cult members believe that the wealth was intended for them by their deities and ancestors. Cargo cults developed primarily in remote parts of New Guinea and other Melanesian and Micronesian societies in the southwest Pacific Ocean, beginning with the first significant arrivals of Westerners in the 19th century. Similar behaviors have, however, also appeared elsewhere in the world.

Cargo cult activity in the Pacific region increased significantly during and immediately after World War II, when the residents of these regions observed the Japanese and American combatants bringing in large amounts of material. When the war ended, the military bases closed and the flow of goods and materials ceased. In an attempt to attract further deliveries of goods, followers of the cults engaged in ritualistic practices such as building crude imitation landing strips, aircraft and radio equipment, and mimicking the behavior that they had observed of the military personnel operating them.

Over the last sixty-five years, most cargo cults have disappeared. However, some cargo cults are still active including:

- The John Frum cult on Tanna island (Vanuatu)
- The Tom Navy cult on Tanna island (Vanuatu)
- The Prince Philip Movement on Tanna island (Vanuatu)
- Yali's cargo cult on Papua New Guinea (Madang-region)
- The Paliau movement on Papua New Guinea (Manus island)
- The Peli association on Papua New Guinea
- The Pomio Kivung on Papua New Guinea

These cults were started by very intelligent people, within their own culture. However, they were dealing with a more advanced culture that did things that appeared to them to be magical and supernatural, just as the UFOs did to our early ancestors. Think about it!

INDEX

A

Adam, 18, 35, 162
Adamski, George, 45
Adapa, 57
Ankerberg, John, 29
Annunaki, 55, 57, 72, 73
Arnold, Kenneth, 11, 16, 31, 33
Arthur C. Clarke's third law, 13

B

Baal, 42, 43
Ba'al Hadad, 40
Bach, Egon, 27
Beck, Fred, 216
Bel, 41
Benevolent Ones, 50
Bessor, John Philip, 31
Beta Israel, 37
Bigfoot, 211, 212, 213, 214, 215, 217, 218, 219, 220, 221, 222, 223, 224
Black Sun, 85, 86, 89, 94
Blumrich, Josef F., 21, 62
B'nai Elohim, 35, 37, 38, 39, 43
Book of Enoch, 37, 38
Book of Exodus, 97
Book of Ezekiel, 21, 22, 62
Book of Genesis, 36
Book of Matthew, 35, 36
Book of Numbers, 39
Book of Parables, 37
Book of the Watchers, 37
Boone, Daniel, 214
Bourne, Geoffrey, 218
British Round Table Group, 92
Brothers of the Light, 86
Brunstein, Karl, 30
Budden, Albert, 28
Bulwer-Lytton, Edward, 85
Burns, J. W., 214

C

Cage, John M., 32
California, Bluff Creek, 215, 216, 217
Campbellin, Bernard G., 219
Canaan, 39, 41, 97
Cargo Cult, 225
Cattle Mutilations, 26
Chariots of the Gods, 22
Childress, David Hatcher, 19
China Lake Naval Weapons Centre, 194
Clark, Jerome, 29
Clarke, David, 33
Coleman, Peter F., 27

'

'Commander X, 126

C

Condon, Edward U., 25
Constable, Trevor James, 31
Cooper, Milton William, 55
Council on Foreign Relations, 92
Crew, Jerry, 216
Crick, Francis, 18

D

Devereux, Paul, 27
Disraeli, Benjamin, 94

E

Ebla civilization, 40
Eden, Jerome, 26
Ēl, 40
Elat, 41
Enoch, 37, 38, 70
Enuma Elish, 73
Eritrean Orthodox Church, 37
Esagila, 73
Ethiopian Orthodox Church, 37
Evans, Hilary, 33, 34
Ezekiel's wheel, 21, 61

F

Fortean Times Magazine, 33

G

Gigantopithecus, 218, 219
Gilgamesh, 42, 197
Gimlin, Robert, 217
Gold, Thomas, 18
Good, Timothy, 139, 140, 196
Goodall, Jane, 212
Gordon, Stan, 223
Goring, Hermann, 88
Green, John William, 216
Greer, Steven, 19
Greys., 45, 186
Grodon, Robert J., 54

H

Hamilton, Pamela, 170
Haushofer, Karl, 86
Helvetius, 74, 75, 76, 77
Heuyer, George, 34
Himmler, Heinrich, 88
Hitler, Adolf, 86, 88
Holy Bible, 21
Hughes, Stephen, 27

Hynek, J. Allen, 30

I

Inner World, 91

J

Jacobs, David Dr., 161, 205
Jenseitsflugmaschine, 90
Jesus Christ, 107, 121
Jung, Carl Gustav, 34

K

Kane, Paul, 213
Keel, John, 27, 29, 30, 177, 223
Keel, John A., 124
Ken Hudnall Show, 102, 147
Kennedy, John F., 54
Keyhoe, Donald, 25
Klass, Philip J., 26
Krantz, Grover, 218, 219
Kronos, 42

L

Leeson, Peter, 224
Livingstone, Harrison Edward, 54
Lords of the Inner Earth, 88
Lummi,, 213

M

Madrid, Miguel DeLa, 168
Magonia Magazine, 33
Marduk, 41, 42, 73
Méheust, Bertrand, 33
Meldrum, Jeffrey, 212
Men in Black, 180, 181, 182
Menger, Howard, 45
MJ 12, 54

Monnerie, Michel, 33
Morell, Theodor Dr., 88
Moses, 97, 98, 100, 101, 102, 103, 104, 105, 106, 112
Mount Lassen, 171
Mount Rainier, 12
Mount St. Helens, 213
MYSTERIOUS AIRSHIP, 81

N

Nephilim, 36, 37, 38, 39, 43, 193, 198
New Mexico, Roswell, 12
New World Order, 91, 93, 94, 185
Noah, 37, 39
Nordic looking aliens, 45

O

Oannes, 11, 12, 56, 57
O'Brien, Cathy, 168
Order of Skull and Bones, 91
Orsic, Maria, 89
Ostman, Albert, 216
Ostrander, Sheila, 52

P

Patterson, Robert, 217
Pennsylvania, Derry, 223
Persinger, Michael, 27
Philosopher's stone, 74
Pinkham, Mark Amaru, 169
Pope, Nick, 19
Presence, 49, 50, 51, 52, 53, 54
Pyle, Robert Michael, 213

R

Reich, William, 26
Reptilians, 161, 164
Rogo, D. Scott, 30

Rund flugzeug, 90

S

Sanderson, Ivan T., 31
Sasquatch, 200, 211, 214, 216, 217, 219
Schroeder, Lynn, 52
Schulmann, W. O., 90
Schweitzer, Johann Friedrich. *See* Helvetius

'

'Serpent People', 126

S

Shadow People', 146
Sheaffer, Robert, 33
Shuker, Karl, 32
Sightings, 182, 183, 215
Sitchin, Zecharia, 17, 56
Slick, Tom, 215
Space Brothers, 50
Spencer, John, 31
Superstition Mountains, 171, 174

T

Tabernacle, 98
Tassili region, 20
The Earth Chronicles, 17
The Spaceships of Ezekiel, 21, 62
Thule, 86, 89, 90, 94
Tonnies, Tonnies, 30
Torah, 97
Trance Formation Of America,, 168
Trent, Eva, 174
Tsoukalos, Giorgio A., 19

V

Vallée, Jacques, 26, 28
Von Däniken, Erich, 17, 19, 22
Vril Gesellschaft, 89
Vril Society., 86

W

Walden, James L., 164
Wallace, Wilbur L., 217

Washington, George, 165
Weldon, John, 29

Y

Yahweh, 37, 38, 39, 42, 97

Z

Zeus, 40, 42

www.ingramcontent.com/pod-product-compliance
Lightning Source LLC
Chambersburg PA
CBHW030316080526
44584CB00012B/588